THE TEA PLANTER'S CHILDREN

Tales from an Indian Childhood

EVE BAKER

Bloomington, IN  Milton Keynes, UK

AuthorHouse™
1663 Liberty Drive, Suite 200
Bloomington, IN 47403
www.authorhouse.com
Phone: 1-800-839-8640

AuthorHouse™ UK Ltd.
500 Avebury Boulevard
Central Milton Keynes, MK9 2BE
www.authorhouse.co.uk
Phone: 08001974150

© 2006 Eve Baker. All rights reserved.

No part of this book may be reproduced, stored in a retrieval system, or transmitted by any means without the written permission of the author.

First published by AuthorHouse 4/13/2006

ISBN: 1-4208-9629-6 (sc)

Printed in the United States of America
Bloomington, Indiana

This book is printed on acid-free paper.

Image Editing and Cover Design by Chris Baker.

INDIA

Far away where the blue hills rise
And crane their heads to reach the skies,
While round their feet the soft mists curl
In gossamer strands the colour of pearl,
And through the valleys silver streams
Wind forever through my dreams.

Far away where those blue hills rise,
That's where my home peacefully lies,
Up on those lovely, rain-washed slopes,
In the land where the black bear lopes
And the jackal howls to the moon.
The land of the summer monsoon.

(By Eve Mc Mullin, aged 11.)

TABLE OF CONTENTS

INTRODUCTION..ix

THE BUNGALOW 1

TIGERS IN THE DARK...7

THE PILGRIMAGE...17

REPOSSESSING SUNNY JIM 33

FIRE-WALKERS AND A MISSIONARY 42

LUNCHING WITH FATHER 51

WAKING FROM DREAMS 60

GARDENS OF REMEMBRANCE 66

UNSUITABLE PETS 71

JOURNEY TO NARGACOIL....................................81

THE NIGHT OF THE VAMPIRE 95

DISH OF THE DAY...100

JACKO 114

THE SLEEPING PRINCE 121

THE JUJU CAT 126

EXPEDITIONS 132

DISCOVERIES..140

THE FALL 149

CONCERNING ELEPHANTS 164

THE MONSOON	169
CHRISTMAS	183
THE LETTER	189
THE VOYAGE HOME	201
GOING BACK	210

INTRODUCTION

At two a.m. one night in March 1925, by the light of a hurricane lantern, a servant was sent hurrying four miles from the bungalow of an Indian tea estate to fetch the doctor, for everything indicated that I was about to be born.

I was the third of four children, and part of the fourth generation of Father's family to be born in India. His forebears were soldiers in the Indian Army. Like them, he had been sent back to England as a young child to be educated but at eighteen he joined the Army and served in South Africa during the second Boer War.

He stayed on in Africa for a while after the war and tried his hand at various unsuccessful business enterprises such as breeding greyhounds and running a general store, then moved on to work on a rubber plantation in Ceylon. Those were pioneering days, where young men were encouraged to try to make their fortunes in the Colonies. Conditions were very harsh in an area remote and malaria infested, and this undoubtedly affected his health for the rest of his life.

He came back to Britain in 1914, to re-enlist and served with the Yorkshire Light Infantry in France, but he returned to Ceylon after the Armistice, this time to grow tea and coffee.

In many ways possessed of a similar spirit of adventure to Father's, Mother had visited India for a short time just before the 1914 war, travelling to Poona with a family as their daughter's governess. She had been educated at a Belgian convent and spoke French fluently, and had also learnt to drive almost at the advent of the motor car. For a time she was employed as governess/ chauffeur for £20 a year!

Through the 1914 War, after a period as an unpaid probationer at a convalescent home for wounded officers, she became a VAD and drove a van to deliver newspapers and letters to the military hospitals in France and Belgium.

Later she acted as personal secretary to the ballerina, Anna Pavlova, whenever she was performing in London. They corresponded after Mother went back to the East, and Pavlova was godmother to my sister.

She was thirty two when, after the war, she came to Ceylon to visit her elder sister, who was married to the manager of a rubber plantation in the district where Father was working. She came to get over a broken romance, and that was where she met and married Father. Later she was to remark that she came for six months, but stayed fourteen years!

It was after their marriage that Father was appointed manager of Arnakal, 3,000 feet up in the Cardamon Hills in what was then known as the state of Travencore. Temperamentally they were opposites, Mother being by nature an optimist, out-going and vivacious, where Father, six years her senior, was shy, introverted and subject to moods of depression, caused by ill-health, but alleviated by his sense of humour.

Tea Planters were allowed home leave only every four or five years. In 1931, after spending a year on leave in England with our parents, my younger brother Peter and I came back to Arnakal with them, but Robert and Ann, our elder siblings, who were of school age, had been left behind at boarding schools. Since there was no air travel, and the sea-voyage took several weeks, we did not expect to see them again until Father's next leave in not less than four years time. Although this was the accepted custom at that time, it was distressing both for them and for Mother.

On that next leave it was expected that I and probably Peter would join Robert and Ann at their schools, and be left behind in England with them. However, circumstances decreed that we were to escape that particular trauma.

The stories that follow concern the three years after our return without the older children that lead to our final unexpected departure in 1934. It describes a time and life-style that was particular to us, living as we did in a remote place with only a small and scattered European population.

Aged four and six on our return, Peter and I were dimly aware that in the outside world there was someone called 'Herr Hitler' who was being what Father called a 'ruddy nuisance'; while in India, Ghandi, not yet recognised by the British as the great patriot and revered figure he was to become, always seemed to be fasting in order to get his own way.

We heard our parents talk of the problems in Britain of the unemployed ex-service men, of the dole queues and the urgent need for a solution. However, as children we were, naturally, engrossed in our own affairs and only vaguely conscious of the world outside.

Later, after we left India, being very homesick for the place where I had lived for the first nine years of my life, in my dreams I would return there and wander through the gardens and the house at Arnakal, reliving our adventures, some of which I now relate.

I have altered the names of the people we knew, because, though most are long gone, they, no doubt, had descendants whose privacy must be respected. Many of the attitudes expressed are no longer PC, but, however wrong or even shocking they may seem today, they were what was accepted at the time of which I write, and in no way express my present views.

Of course the stories are only what I myself recall after a lifetime of absence. Peter's memories may sometimes differ from mine and will of course be from another perspective. All four of us, the Tea Planter's children, have always looked back on our life at Arnakal as a time of great happiness, and tranquillity. For our parents, too, it was the happiest time of their lives.

As a postscript to the stories, I have described how Peter and I returned to Arnakal in 1998 on a sentimental journey to discover some extraordinary coincidences, and many remnants of the life we remembered.

THE BUNGALOW

The bungalow in which we lived was situated a little below the crest of a small hill, surrounded by other hills which rose into the blue distance on every side, ridged with terraces of tea, or forested with jungle and bamboo. It sprawled at the end of an avenue of feathery acacia trees leading to the factory and the village.

First there were the big green wooden gates on which Peter and I used to swing. Then came the garage with its tall faded green doors. Within the garage there was a cement pit where the engineer would work when the car needed repairing, and sometimes toads would gather and become trapped. No one could understand how or why they were there. Peter and I carried them out, (twenty-three on one occasion!) and put them on the rockery outside the nursery veranda. There they croaked all night. Peter and I told each other they were singing a song of gratitude.

Past the garage, past the patch of lilies that never flowered, in what was regarded as my garden, the lawns curved away as the gravel drive, source of many a grazed knee, opened out into a broad crescent before the house.

The garden was laid out in terraces reached by stone steps under pergolas of roses or a creeper with orange honeysuckle like flowers. Opposite the house was a tennis court made of red laterite, and overlooking the court, but rooted beyond the wire-netting fence, grew a mahogany tree, a tall bare trunk with a cluster of branches at the very top. It had been planted by the original owner of Arnakal when first he came there, in the eighteen-nineties. Every year it dropped one branch and grew a bit taller. Peter and I would stare up at it and try to guess how far it would reach if it fell. Would it reach to the bungalow? we wondered.

Almost the whole house was circled by a wide, red-flagged veranda, with paved steps leading up to it from between raised beds that were always full of nasturtiums and petunias. The house was raised on its foundations to prevent flooding during the monsoon. Where the house faced the gates, the veranda was shielded by a glass and timber screen, which sheltered it from wind and rain. Here our parents would sit with friends who came to play tennis or bridge, and pass the evening before dinner, drinking whisky-and-soda chotapegs. It was here that Mother gave Peter and me our morning lessons. We would sit up at the gate-legged table with our exercise books, making pot-hooks and hangers as we learned to write. If we shaped our letters well, she would reward us by dotting in eyes, noses and mouths to turn them into faces.

The house, not beautiful or architecturally distinguished, had a pleasant appearance. Beneath the cheerfully red-tiled roof, the veranda stretched out each side like welcoming arms. The rooms within were bright and airy; all the walls were white-washed, reflecting back the light from the many windows.

The Bungalow

The sitting room lay behind the screened part of the veranda, at the front of house; a large room with a bay window at one end and a stone fireplace at the other. Most of the furniture belonged with the house, but Mother had added touches of her own, such as the tulip patterned chintz curtains and the cushions on the window seat which she had made with her sewing machine. Vases, books and brass ornaments furnished the tables and shelves round the room. A bearskin rug and the skins of two pythons lay on the floor, and in the evenings a log fire blazed in the fireplace.

The dining room led out of the sitting room. It was filled by a long polished table. There was a grandfather clock in one corner that chimed the hours, and a sideboard against one wall, on which stood a silver tantalus with cut-glass decanters. Hunting prints decorated the walls, and a picture, painted by a friend of Mother's, of a sunset over marshland. It was a dark picture, the only light being the sky reflected in the marshy pools, which to me resembled a black and white dog. In fact I could never see it as other than a picture of a dog.

On the dining table, which was for the purpose moved on to the veranda, because of the need for maximum light, Father had nine inches of his duodenum removed by Dr Somervell, of Everest fame. It was an emergency, as his ulcer had perforated, and there was no time for the journey to hospital in Nargacoil, where my tonsils had been removed, as it would have involved travelling some hundred miles down the ghat and across the coastal plain. A telegram was sent to Dr Somervell, who, in spite of having malaria at the time, drove from Vallore with his nurse and saved Father's life.

The bungalow was always called 'The New Bungalow', for it had been built on the site of the 'Old Bungalow' while we were on leave, but made to face in a new direction. The Old Bungalow faced north, perhaps for reasons of coolness, but was therefore rather dark and gloomy. The New Bungalow was superior in several ways, but mainly because it had flush lavatories as opposed to the commodes and chamber pots we had managed with before. It was wired for electric light, but the generator that was to have powered the lights was never acquired, so oil lamps were the only source of illumination, while the electric sockets dangled empty from the ceilings of all the rooms. There were, however, electric bells, running off a car battery in the roof, with which to summon the servants.

There was a bathroom for each bedroom, including the two guest-rooms, and one leading off Father's dressing room. All were equipped with wooden washstands with china jugs and basins, and painted wooden baths resting in shallow cement sinks with drainage holes through the wall. When baths were needed Kunichin, the house-boy, or Francis, the butler would bring cans of hot water to fill the tub. The cans were empty kerosene tins, with a piece of wood nailed across the top for a handle: the standard bucket in India, where nothing was ever wasted.

Our mother's bathroom had a door leading to the nursery veranda so that if we had bad dreams or needed her in the night, she could hear us call, and would hurry across to comfort us, candle or torch in hand, picking her way through the scattered toys.

The high wooden beds stood with their feet in tins of water to discourage the termites. All the static furniture in the house was similarly protected. Termites could eat their way, unobserved, into the heart of the wood, leaving the outside layer intact until suddenly the whole thing would collapse into a heap of dust. However, they could not swim, hence the water pots.

In a storeroom off the main corridor all the china and glass were kept, and the brass oil lamps were put away during the day. Here, each day they were filled and polished before being placed in all the rooms at dusk.

Leading from the pantry was a small room that contained a bale of raw cotton. Once a year, one by one the mattresses were taken from the beds and laid on sheets of hessian on the gravel terrace. There the seams would be opened and all the lumps that had developed in the cotton lint were picked apart, and handfuls of fresh cotton from the bale were added. Then Mother would stitch the seams together again, and with a long needle threaded with string, sew short strips of cloth to 'button' the filling in place and keep it from shifting.

The kitchen was separated from the house by a covered way. How any food arrived hot is a mystery, after its long journey from the kitchen to the table. Cooking was done on a wood-fired stove. Muthu, the cook, spoke no English, so Francis had to translate for Mother. He was, however, an excellent cook and made the lightest sponges I have ever eaten.

The servants had their rooms on the shady side of the kitchen, facing the yard where the poultry scratched during the day. There was a chopping block where logs were split for the stove, and chickens were beheaded before being prepared for cooking. Peter and I would hang about in the kitchen, watching coconut being grated on a piece of tin nailed to a log, or rice being pounded in a big wooden mortar. Sometimes the servants let me sip their coffee, very black, sweetened with jaggery sugar. We children were not allowed to drink coffee, and I still remember how delicious I found the hot syrupy forbidden drink.

This, then was our home, though the word 'Home' was always used by our parents and the other Europeans to mean England, a mysterious far-away place where Robert and Ann were at school and we had all stayed during that last leave. Peter and I knew that one day we too would be left there to go to school, something I found hard to imagine, even though at that time I could not know that our return to England would be forever. I had consoled myself with the certainty that when our education was complete, we would come back to live at Arnakal with our parents.

TIGERS IN THE DARK

Our mother and father were about to leave for the Club. Mother was wearing her beaded black evening dress and carried a shawl over her arm in case it was cool when she returned. She came to find us to say 'goodbye'.

"They can have their baths now," she told Ayah, our Indian nanny, "then they can go in their pyjamas with you to Munjamully to take Peggy back ."

Overjoyed, we hugged her. "Can we really? Hooray ! Mmm! You smell of scent ! Lovely!"

The party that night was in honour of Peggy's parents, former managers of a neighbouring tea plantation. A year or two ago, they had moved to an estate in the High Range, some hundred or so miles away. As with our family, their two eldest children were at school in England, so when they returned to visit the Cargils, who managed Munjamully, the next estate to ours, Peggy stayed with us in order that she would have the company of other children. Her parents had been popular in the District, and the party was to say farewell for they were leaving at daybreak to return to High Range.

"Now promise me you will be good and come straight back with Ayah," Mother said, "You mustn't stop and play when you get there or you won't get back before dark. Ayah, remember to take the torch, in case you need it on the way home."

"Yes ! Yes ! We promise !" we said, following her to the car and climbing on the running board to kiss our parents 'goodbye'. "Let us ride up the hill, Daddy." We begged, pulling Peggy up beside us.

Laughing, Father agreed and drove slowly and carefully through the gates and up the avenue towards the tea factory and main road. We hung on to the open windows of the car until it reached the top of the hill, then jumped off and waved as, gathering speed, it whirled out of sight in a cloud of white dust, whereupon we raced each other back to the bungalow, where the houseboy had already filled the green and white painted wooden bath with hot water, and Ayah was laying out our towels and pyjamas.

At seven, a year older than me, Peggy was a pretty child with a sophistication lacking in my brother Peter and myself. For example, she declared that she no longer believed in fairies. Peter and I were shocked, for we loved fairies too much to relinquish our faith in them easily. At the same time, we did not want to be thought babyish, so we listened in silence to her blasphemy !

She had also shown me how to smoke, with a cigarette taken from her mother's case. We hid in the furthest corner of the garden, not answering when Peter called us. Again she shocked me, by stealing from her mother, but all the same I had a delicious sense of sin as we passed the cigarette back and forth, blowing out the smoke in a thin white stream, as grown ups did.

Bath time that night was accomplished with some impatience from Ayah, and much giggling and splashing from us. We did not much like this Ayah, but dared not disobey her because she threatened us with foul tortures and had been known to pinch very painfully on several occasions. Before her there had been the beloved Old Ayah, who had arrived for the birth of my eldest brother, and been the centre of our lives until our last leave. Since our parents could not afford to take her to England with us, she had gone to another family . On our return, minus our elder brother and sister, this present Ayah had come to look after us .

On this night, we all got into the bath together, and in the confusion of arms and legs, Ayah was unsure whether she had washed all the knees, or some twice, and some not at all!

At length, pyjamaed and dressing gowned, having eaten our supper we set out to walk the two miles to Munjamully to take Peggy back. Peggy and I ran ahead to climb the stile to the footpath we were to take, while Ayah struggled after us with Peggy's suitcase and Peter in the pushchair. Our sandalled feet were very quiet on the mossy path, while the gum trees throbbed with cicadas. We followed the contour of the hill, past an outcrop of huge rocks . Trees had taken root in some of the fissures, so that the rocks, from a distance, looked like elephants with green howdahs on their backs, gazing down at the waterfalls in the valley below. Our plantation was called Arnakal, which in Tamil means Elephant Rock.

Reaching the road, our little party of children in our bright dressing gowns, trailed on, stopping here and there to stroke the leaves of sensitive plants to see them close. Peggy and I took turns to carry her case, when Ayah began to grumble, with some justification, that she could not manage it and the pushchair. Peter sat, allowing himself to be wheeled along while he watched the changing colours of the terraced hills as the shadows lengthened.

Just before the turning to Munjamully, we passed a patch of eta grass growing right to the edge of the road, dense and full of shadows.

"There are tigers in there." said Peggy, casually, "My Mummy told me."

"Are there really?" I asked, staring nervously through the pale stems. The sun streaked shadows looked very much like the stripes of lurking tigers ! I was reluctant to look too closely, in case I saw one.

"Yes," Peggy went on confidently," It's the sort of place that tigers like to hide in. One killed a coolie coming back from the bazaar last week."

"Really?" I said, surprised that such sensational news had not reached me before. "Are you sure?"

"Oh yes ! My Ayah told me. Come on, I'll race you to the house."

Peter was allowed to join us as we all three ran up the drive to the Cargil's house, arriving hot and breathless, with Ayah trailing behind with the suitcase in the pushchair. We were greeted by the grey haired houseboy, Joseph. All the grown ups were at the Club, and Peggy's Ayah was in the garden mending clothes.

Tigers in the Dark

"Can we have some lemonade, please ?" Peggy asked, and Joseph went away to get it.

Ayah sat down thankfully beside Peggy's Ayah and said: "Now you must not be long, because it will soon be getting dark, and I forgot the torch."

We drank our lemonade and ran off to explore the garden. Full of shady corners and large flowering shrubs, it was a wonderful place for hide-and-seek, and we soon forgot the time. Ayah, too, was enjoying herself, with another ayah to talk to and a chance to compare notes on their employers and their children, and she too forgot that time was passing. When at last she called us, we were engrossed in our game and it was some time before we were all assembled .

"Come, "said Ayah," We must go home quickly now, or it will be dark and there will be tigers."

Already the daylight was fading, and in half an hour it would be gone. The mention of tigers reminded me of Peggy's tale when we had stopped by the eta patch.

"We must have a torch!" I said, "It's getting dark now. Why didn't you bring it, Ayah?"

"YOU should have remembered, Eve !" Ayah said crossly, " I have too much to remember !"

Joseph was unhelpful when approached. His English was not as good as that of our own servants. The Cargils spoke Tamil fluently, and therefore had not required English as a qualification when choosing their staff . Old Joseph spoke better English than the rest of the household, but I was not sure that he fully understood our needs.

"We want to borrow a torch, please, Joseph." I said.

"No, Missy, no can find." he said.

Ayah was afraid of the dark, and afraid of the wrath of our parents. She knew that she should not have allowed us to stay so long and that she had spent too long chatting to Peggy's Ayah, but it had been a treat to have another woman to talk to. She began to scold us .

Ignoring her, Peter and I asked when the Cargils and Peggy's parents would be back.

"Ten...twelve o'clock." was the reply.

"But we must go home!" we repeated." Can't someone come with a lantern?"

All the time we had been speaking, the servants had been busy in the scullery, filling and trimming the oil lamps and were beginning to place them in the rooms and passages.

"There is no one." said Joseph, unhelpfully.

"We cannot go in the dark," said Ayah, "There will be tigers in the dark. At night there are always tigers. You should have come sooner, disobedient children !"

Peter and I knew that Ayah and the other servants threatened us with tigers just to hurry us on, but Peggy's words about the eta jungle that I knew we would have to pass, had brought a frisson of fear, of which I knew our mother would disapprove. She always laughed at the idea of bogeymen and night terrors, taking us into the garden to look at the stars so that we should not be afraid at night.

"There aren't any tigers," I said, with a firmness that belied my feeling of panic, "We can't stay here. We were told to go home."

By now it was totally dark outside. The oil lamps glowed in the house. Peggy was having cocoa and biscuits before she went to bed. We were invited to join her. When

Tigers in the Dark

we had finished we went to the kitchen and I approached Joseph firmly.

"Joseph, you MUST lend us a lantern !"

"No, Missy, no lantern. All needed here."

"We can send it back tomorrow," I reasoned, "Mr Cargil won't mind."

Joseph, I think, disliked children, and felt that we had brought our misfortunes on ourselves. Peter was beginning to look tearful. It was past his bed time and he could see no hope of getting home.

"We can't go in the dark!" he wailed.

"I know!" I said, trying to imagine how our parents would deal with the situation.

Normally, at home, we were not allowed to issue orders to the servants in the way I had been doing, but I was trying to imitate my parents in order to get Joseph to co-operate. In fact, I was certainly antagonising him further. I had a sudden inspiration.

"I know," I said, "You must send someone to the Club to tell Mummy."

"No one can go, Missy," he said, slowly polishing glasses and arranging them on a tray. "Too dark...all go home ."

"Someone must take a lantern and go!" I repeated determinedly.

"Yes, Missy," said Joseph, continuing with his task.

"Please, Joseph, please." I said, "please send someone... can't the gardener go?"

"Gone home now, "he said.

Tears were beginning to sting my eyes, and Peter was snivelling .

"You've got to go!" he shouted at a youth who was cleaning the lamp table. "Why won't you go?"

But Joseph only said, "Yes, yes. Very good. Very good." And the boy at the table laughed and mimicked, "Very good, Missy." but neither of them made a move.

We went back to the sitting room and discussed how long it would take a man on a bicycle to reach the Club, and for our mother to return. Peggy, who had to be up at dawn, had gone to bed, and her Ayah had gone for her evening meal. Our Ayah sat with her hands folded in her lap and muttered about how naughty we were and that it was time we too were in bed, asleep. Joseph stood in the doorway and watched us. I knew that if my father had spoken in the tone I had tried to imitate, there would have been instant action, but my words were ignored. I stopped listening to Ayah's complaints.

The moon had risen and the clouds that had hidden the stars blew apart in the night breeze. It was a brilliant night.

"Do you think," asked Peter, "that if we shout as loud as we can, they would hear us at the Club?"

"I don't know." I said, "let's try."

It seemed better than sitting doing nothing, so we ran across the garden to the end of a terrace that overlooked the valley where the Club was situated, two miles away. We filled our lungs and opened our mouths wide to shout as loudly as we could.

"Mummeeee!....Mummeeeee! Come ba-a-ack!" we screamed.

The sound echoed back from the surrounding hills, and far away, dogs began to bark. Again and again we

Tigers in the Dark

screamed our message into the night. We were quite unaware of anything except the need for our mother.

The garden was black and silver in the moonlight, and the stillness, when we ceased our din to listen for a reply, struck our ears with a silence that was full of small distant noises: of crickets winding their watches, the thin high squeak of bats, and distant barking. We began to feel the cold through our thin cotton dressing gowns, so we went back to the house and stood on the veranda and shouted until our voices began to croak. Ayah sat clicking her tongue in disapproval, but at the same time hoping that someone would come and rescue us. It was past the time of her evening meal, and she was hungry.

A long time seemed to pass while we shouted and bawled together, and then we heard the sound of an engine on the hill, and headlights sent beams flashing through the trees. There was the sound of wheels crunching on the gravel, and voices. We ran to meet the car as Mother climbed out and came towards us.

"Oh, Mummy, Mummy!" we cried hoarsely as we flung our arms round her.

"Hello, you naughty scamps!" she said, "What are you doing here at this time of night?"

"It got too dark, and Ayah forgot the torch, and we were afraid of the tiger, and we didn't know what to do.... They wouldn't give us a lantern..."

Ayah had followed us out and stood nervously behind us.

"Madam, I tell them to come, but they will not!" she said "They do not listen to me. Please Madam, I try to take them home, but then it is too dark, and I am afraid tigers will be coming."

"All right Ayah," said Mother, annoyed that she should be so bad at controlling us. "Mr Cargil has very kindly driven me here to see what was wrong. Now we are going to take you home, and then we will go back to the Club."

Relieved and chastened we got into the car. As we drove back we asked if they had heard us calling.

"Somebody passing said there was a terrible row going on at Munjamully," said Mother, laughing, "so we came to see what was happening."

"We thought tigers would eat us !"said Peter sleepily

"There aren't any tigers," said Mother, reassuringly, "except in the jungle."

"Peggy said there were," I said, "she said one killed a man from the bazaar."

"What nonsense." said Mother, "One got a goat over at Peermade ages ago, but I think it was shot."

Safely in bed with the mosquito net tucked in, I dreamed of a tiger licking his paws as he sat in the white dust of the road, and waited for Ayah.

THE PILGRIMAGE

The idea had developed during the day after our morning lesson with Mother. The subject had been pilgrims, beginning with the Canterbury Tales and Chaucer's Pilgrims, but continuing with many variants on this theme, particularly those along the road to Benares and the shores of the great Ganges. These were the ones that most appealed to us, for they were, in a sense, a part of the fabric of life in India even in a largely Christian state like Travancore. We had heard of the holy men who measured their length for mile after mile to the Ganges; and others who held one arm above their heads until it atrophied. I had tried this once, but after a few minutes it ached so much that I was forced to lower it.

"They take a vow," Mother told us, "in the hope that they will be forgiven some of the bad things they have done. Or, sometimes so that God will grant them a favour for the rest of mankind."

In the village there was a little girl, younger than we were, whose hair hung to her shoulders in a matted mass. As a baby she had been very ill, close to death. Her parents had vowed that if she recovered, they would never wash or comb her hair. I thought it was unkind of her parents to make such a promise on her behalf, and could not understand why God should want her to do it. She would have been so much prettier and more comfortable with her hair oiled and combed into shining plaits like the other village girls.

Mother said she thought it was good to set oneself hard tasks and make oneself carry them out. It was probably this last remark which began it.

During our afternoon rest, we discussed this and tried to think of a hard task we could set ourselves. We thought we should carry something heavy night and day, but it seemed to us that that would make ordinary life impossible.

"We couldn't do anything," Peter pointed out, "our hands would be full."

Somehow the idea of a journey began to take root, and I had the idea that we should carry water with us in bottles. That would be our burden, and it would be useful too, because we could drink it if we were thirsty. Somehow the need for food did not occur to us, but at that stage we were still theorising.

"The bottles would be a bit of a nuisance," said Peter, ever practical.

"It's supposed to be a Pilgrimage !" I said, "It's meant to be hard."

We decided that we would acquire a bottle each and tie it to a stick. This we could carry over one shoulder, which we felt would make it easier.

We went in search of bottles. These were valued commodities, and there was considerable opposition from Francis and Kunichin, the house servants. The soda bottles always went back to the Club to be refilled, and the beer and whisky bottles were also either returned or re-used in the kitchen. In the end, Mother was appealed to, and she allowed us a bottle each, provided we promised not to break them.

This was the day when she left us for the afternoon and went to the Club to play tennis, leaving us in the care of the servants. The Ayah we had had on our return from leave in England, had proved unsatisfactory. Mother decided that she could look after us herself, with the help of the house servants. We were unusual at that time, in not having an ayah, and as a result had a far greater freedom than most European children.

As he gave us the bottles, Francis demanded indignantly: "Why do you want them ?"

"We want to put water in them," said Peter.

"Why, Master Peter?"

We were reluctant to discuss our idea, and embarrassed to explain to Christian Francis that we were imitating Hindu holy men.

"We're going on a journey," I said, "And we need the water to drink on the way."

"Where you go then ?" Francis asked suspiciously.

"We're being pilgrims," said Peter.

"We're going a long way away." I said firmly. "And we're going on our own."

This last remark was in order that neither of the servants would follow us. Even as I spoke, the idea began to take root. Why not? We would travel as far as we could, and find out how far we could get alone. I imagined our return years later, after traversing India, being greeted like the Prodigal son.

"Where?" Francis was equally firm. "You must not go unless you tell me where, Missy."

"We're. . .We're going to the Gilbeys." I said in another burst of inspiration. The Gilbeys lived at Mount, a neighbouring tea estate, several miles away. They were close friends of our parents and although childless, they were fond of children, and always made us welcome when we visited. However, we had never walked there. Nor had we ever walked anywhere like as far, but the idea appealed to me, and Peter seemed willing to co-operate.

"No, no." said Francis, "it is too far. What you do when it getting dark? Your Mummy will be angry."

"No, she won't mind. Really, Francis. It's a pilgrimage, you see."

Francis called Kunichin, the houseboy, who had been standing nearby, grinning. He was amused by our ambitious plans, which he did not take seriously. He and Francis conversed in Tamil so we should not understand what they said.

Turning back to us, Francis said, "Kunichin go with you."

We groaned. The last thing we wanted was Kunichin's company. He would spoil everything; mocking us if we gave up; grumbling if we went too far, and, of course, reporting everything back to Francis, who, in turn would tell our parents all our misdeeds.

"No ! Kunichin can't come. You must stay here, Kunichin, do you hear?" we commanded.

But as we set off, the bottles swaying uncomfortably on the end of bamboo canes held over our shoulders, he followed at a distance.

The Pilgrimage

After Ayah left, Kunichin had been appointed our minder. He had first come as a small boy, when our elder brother and sister were babies, and in the beginning had been employed to help Old Ayah. He and Robert had become close friends. He had taught Robert how to fly his kite, and how to whip his top until it spun so fast that it seemed to be standing still. Now he was a young adolescent, subject to the unpredictable moods of his age, and had little patience with our fanciful ideas. His duties were mainly those of chokera, or houseboy, under Francis' strict eye, and he resented having to mind us. It was not man's work. However sometimes he would unbend, and on one memorable occasion, he unwound his turban to show me how he made it. Yard after yard after yard of fine white cloth unravelled around him, until it was all undone. Then he began to fold it about his head again. Swiftly and dextrously he wound it back into a tight, neat oval, crossing the folds in a perfect herring bone pattern at the front and back, and tucking the end away deftly, so that it could not unwind again. All without aid of a mirror. To our disappointment, he refused to repeat the performance for Peter, who had arrived on the scene just as the end was tucked in.

We ran out of the garden and joined the path along the other side of the valley. To reach the Gilbeys, we must take the road to the dam, which was a familiar walk for us. Thereafter we would cross the bridge at the far end of the lake, passing a stretch of jungle.

This, again, was familiar, for sometimes we walked a little way in through the trees with Mother. When she and Father had first moved to Arnakal, they had explored that patch of jungle. On one of their expeditions a bear had leapt up out of a clump of long grass just in front of them. Luckily it took fright and bolted away from them. Had it had a cub with it, it would have been extremely dangerous. There were also herds of wild boar, fearsome creatures with tusks, which roamed through the undergrowth.

The road skirted the jungle through grassy hills with great outcrops of rock, and tufts of citronella grass, which smelt of lemon, but could cut the skin to draw blood. This would be unfamiliar country to us, though we had, of course, been driven through it when we were taken on visits by our parents. This, I thought, would be where the real adventure would begin, but I was sure we could find the way.

As we followed the path along the contour of the hill, we glanced back. There was Kunichin, following faithfully at a distance. His teeth gleamed in his dark face, matching the whiteness of his shirt and dhoti in the sunshine as he grinned at us.

We ran on under an avenue of cedars, whose deep shade was cool and refreshing, turning my white muslin dress to pale green. Across the valley we could see, past a clump of tall, yellow-stemmed bamboos to where the bungalow lay in the late afternoon sun. A wide red-tiled roof above white walls, with a thick bar of darkness which was the veranda. The lawns, sloping away from the house, were splashed with scarlet cannas.

A sudden agitation began in the bushes ahead of us, and a black dog emerged, panting, tail awag in greeting.

The Pilgrimage

"Oh no! Not Digger. . .Go home Digger!" We groaned. How could we go on with our pilgrimage with the dog in tow?

We turned to where Kunichin was trailing behind us and ordered the dog, with what we hoped were firm gestures, to go to Kunichin. Perhaps we could get rid of them both at once.

"Take Digger home, Kunichin," we said, but Kunichin only laughed and shook his head.

Above the cedars lived our nearest neighbour, our father's junior assistant, Mr Wilshaw. His predecessor we had called 'Uncle Benison,' but Mr Wilshaw remained 'Mr'.

At the bottom of the path to his house was a huge iron wheel above a cistern. Every evening water was pumped from the dam to fill the cistern, and from there the gardener turned the wheel to pump the water up to the house.

Resigned to the company of Kunichin and the dog, we marched on. The bottles on the ends of the sticks swung and banged uncomfortably against us as we went. They were indeed a burden and weighed heavily on our shoulders, but we were not to be defeated yet. After all, this was a pilgrimage.

The path wound on round the hillside. The upper slopes, once we left the cedars, were ridged and terraced, covered with neat rows of tea bushes, like green candlewick. On the other side of the path, a jungly scrub fell steeply to where a rocky stream flowed. We were nearing the dam now.

Beside the path ran an iron pipe, supported on wooden posts about a foot high, to ensure an even fall. When

Peter saw it, he climbed up on to the pipe, his bottle of water swinging like a pendulum as he tried to balance along its length. He swayed, one arm stretched sideways, the other holding the bamboo, ran a few steps and fell, landing awkwardly on his knees. The bottle which had destabilised him, lay in smithereens on the path. I ran to help him up.

"You've lost your water." I said, unhelpfully.

He bit back the tears as he nursed his knees. They were only slightly grazed, so he rubbed them with his handkerchief and got up. We gathered up the broken glass from the path so that passing coolies would not cut their feet, and hid the pieces in the stump of a dead tea bush. By now, forgetful of my vow, I had decided that I had had enough of carrying my bottle. We both drank from it before depositing it in the stump with the broken pieces. The afternoon sun had warmed it to an unpleasant luke-warmness. The sticks we kept as staves.

"Pilgrims always carry staves," we agreed, "to help them walk."

Kunichin had caught up with us, and was waiting to see what our next move was to be.

Before us lay the dam; a great grey cement cliff, falling steeply to the rocks fifty feet or so below. There was a dip in the centre for the sluice, but as it was the dry season, there was no cascade over the rim. On the contrary, the dam was in need of repair, and from a crack half way down the wall a thin trickle of water was oozing, streaks of green moss and one or two ferns at its edges. It was some weeks since we had come that way, and we were amazed to see how far the level of the water in the reservoir had fallen. There was some water still behind the barrier, but the large pipe that led to the pump-house was exposed for most of its length, and at the further end of the lake, there were now, instead of water, great banks of silt and reeds.

Ignoring Kunichin, we called Digger, who had walked out along the pipe to drink, and continued on along the road beside the lake. Once more we were entering the coolness of shade; this time in the mottled shadows of a grove of gum trees. Across the road, between the smooth trunks, the hill was a blue mist of flowers above which fluttered myriads of butterflies. Sometimes we brought a net here to catch new specimens to add to our collection.

Once more, we broke into a run, hoping to shake off the doggedly faithful Kunichin. We heard him calling, but we took no notice.

At the far end the lake narrowed to a channel, crossed by a log bridge, beneath which the water in normal circumstances, flowed through marshes and finally ran back towards the plains. Now it was almost dry.

Ahead lay the Gilbeys' house, and we could see the beginning of the jungle. We were hot and sticky from running and growing tired. Our enthusiasm for our adventure was waning. Added to which we were intrigued by what had become of the lake.

At this end it was non-existent, having been replaced by banks of black mud, whose surface had dried and cracked to form grey scabs, and were dotted with tufts of reeds. Veins of liquid mud separated the banks into islands amongst which clumps of marsh flowers had sprung up. Digger was already racing across the mud, eagerly following new smells.

"I think I'll pick some of those flowers for Mummy." I said, forgetting the long pilgrimage I had meant this expedition to be.

"All right. Me too." said Peter.

We sat down and removed our sandals, which we left by the bridge. Then we set forth, gingerly testing the surface with every step, probing the ground ahead with our bamboos.

Kunichin, who had by now caught up, called after us: "No, no, Missy! No, Master Peter, it is not safe. You must not go."

"Don't be silly," we called back. "It's quite safe. We're being careful."

We wandered among the reeds, picking flowers as we went. Peter soon gave this up and went off on an adventure of his own, pretending there were pirates lurking about, or some such thing. Now and then the crust would give way and we would sink a little way into the warm mud. Each time our hearts would lurch in case it was quagmire, but each time it only reached up to our ankles. We lost sight of Kunichin by the bridge as we roamed deeper in amongst the reeds, towards the middle of the lake, leaping over the narrow streams of liquid mud, wading cautiously through the wider ones. Eventually I came to a mud channel some five or six feet wide. Beyond it lay a large island where the flowers seemed more profuse and larger than elsewhere. Testing the depth with my bamboo, I began to cross. The mud rapidly rose above my ankles to my calves, and almost to my knees. I lifted my feet high with each step, the black, evil-smelling mud dripping from them before I sank them back into the mire. I was very nervous, for I had been told of bogs where people sank, never to be seen again, but to my relief, the mud grew shallow again and I reached the other side safely. I picked a few flowers and explored the island, but the reeds were so tall and thick that I could see nothing but the sky, so, turning back, I recrossed the channel again. My dress was by now streaked and splashed with dirt, and I was aware of mud splashes on my face as well. I found Peter on the other shore.

"That's a huge island." I said.

"Did you cross that stream?" he asked.

"Yes, but it's a bit deep. Look at my legs ! I'm wearing gum-boots." We laughed uproariously.

"I'm wearing black shoes and socks." Peter said, looking down at his own legs. Still laughing, he said: "Where did you cross? I want to go there, too."

"Just about there, by those reeds." I said. "It gets quite deep at first, and then shallow again." And without another thought, I set off to explore in a new direction.

I had gone a little way, when suddenly I heard Peter call. There was a note of panic in his voice.

"Eve. . .Eve, quick! Help. I'm stuck."

I ran back, jumping over ditches and dodging through the reeds until I reached him.

There I stopped in dismay at what I saw. Peter was several inches shorter than I was, as was to be expected since he was two years younger, but even allowing for that, I could see that things had gone wrong. He must have picked a different crossing point, for there he was, almost half way across, up to his waist in black sludge, holding his arms clear of the mud. His face showed how scared he was.

The Tea Planter's Children

I thought quickly, and remembering my own crossing, urged: "It gets shallow again the other side. Go on, Peter, it'll be all right."

"Are you sure?" he said, near to tears. But when he tried to move, he only sank deeper.

"How about crawling out?" I suggested, desperate to find a solution quickly, and having some dim recollection of the need to spread the load. . or was that for ice?

"No, no. I can't move. I'm sinking, Eve. Help me, please help me ! Quick!"

Terrified, I tried to think what we should do. Around us the afternoon sun shone blandly on, but the shadows of the reeds were lengthening. Digger came running back to us, his coat plastered with mud, obviously enjoying himself. I remembered the bamboo I was holding. Peter had lost his in the mud, but if I held mine out to him, perhaps he could hold on to the end and I could pull him out. I reached forward with the stick and he grasped it as tightly as he could. But his hands were slimy with mud, and when I began to pull, the stick slid out of them. We both began to cry.

Not until then did we remember Kunichin waiting by the bridge. Probably by now, I thought, he would be furious with us, but I began to shout his name, and Peter joined in. I turned and began to run towards him, calling as I ran, and a minute later met him running towards me, his dhoti hitched up between his legs, ready for action. I led him back to Peter as I tried to explain what had happened. On seeing him, he threw up his hands in horror.

"You bad, bad children," he said," I tell you it not safe here. Why you not listen?"

The Pilgrimage

He looked at Peter's mud and tear streaked face as he stood helpless, up to his chest in the hideous black liquid. There was no time to spare. I was sure he was deeper in the mud than when I had left him.

Cautiously Kunichin stepped into the mud which soon rose to his knees. He stopped. He was now far enough in to reach Peter by bending forward. Gripping Peter's thin arms, he began to pull. His hands slipped on the slime that bedaubed most of Peter and he could not hold him.

With wonderful coolness, he paused to wipe them on his loincloth, and tried again.

In my imagination, I had foreseen the terrible possibility that we might not be able to rescue my beloved little brother, knowing that I would be to blame, and wondering how I would break the news to our parents. So my relief when inch by inch, Peter's body began to emerge, was beyond expressing. First his waist and then his legs appeared, until Kunichin swung him, like a black slug, out on to the bank. His shirt and green shorts were a uniform, stinking, greyish, greenish blackness. Kunichin's shirt and loin cloth were likewise smeared and filthy.

Picking Peter up in his arms, he led us to the far shore of the lake, where he found a pool near the bank that was somehow clear and gravel-bottomed. There he washed us, splashing water over our limbs until most of the mud was gone. We took off our clothes and tried, without much success, to clean them in the pool, while Kunichin washed himself. We were sickened by the smell of the mud, though during the excitement of the afternoon we had been able to ignore it.

Kunichin ran back to the bridge to fetch our sandals, for we were forbidden to walk on the roads barefoot, although the garden was deemed safe and free from the anki worms that caused a wasting disease.

In our gratitude to him for rescuing Peter, we felt a sudden deep affection for Kunichin, and thanked him over and over again, as we headed back towards the dam. Digger ran ahead of us, and plunging into the water, swam across to the pump-house.

Peter and I had been told tales of Kunichin's prowess as a swimmer, but had never seen him swim. Now, feeling that Kunichin was being nice to us, we pleaded with him to give us a demonstration. He, himself, no doubt, was tempted, if only for the opportunity to thoroughly cleanse himself, but at first he refused. Finally he relented, and removing his already wet shirt, he dived in and swam gracefully across and back, to our delighted cheers.

The sun was beginning to sink behind the hill, whose shadow now covered most of the lake. When he emerged, dripping from the water, he sent us home ahead of him.

"Go on." He said, "I will come after." For he needed to wring out his dhoti, and modesty forebade that he remove it in front of us.

We crossed the dam wall, I nervously, mostly on my hands and knees, for I was dreadfully afraid of the great drop on one side. Peter, who though younger than I was, was unafraid of heights, ran across ahead of me. As we reached the road, we saw the engineer going into the pump-house to start the engine.

Naked, except for our sandals, we walked home, clutching our filthy clothes and the remaining bottle, which we retrieved from the stump. As we went, the water began to pulse along the pipe, setting up the throbbing sound that was so familiar to us, with the echo coming back from the hills. "Ker-taw. ker-taw. ker-taw.".

The gardener was already turning the wheel by the cistern, his muscles rippling as he bent and stretched, pushing the wheel round and round. He smiled at us and spoke to Kunichin in Tamil, no doubt remarking on our dishevelled nakedness.

"Kunichin," we begged as we neared the house, "You won't tell Mummy, will you? Please. We'll never, never be naughty again. We'll do everything you tell us. Please, Kunichin. We promise."

"No, I won't tell."

"But our clothes. . . What can we do with our clothes? She'll want to know why they're so dirty." In our anxiety over the state of our clothes, the perils of our adventures were forgotten.

"Give them to me. I will wash them, don't worry." He said with uncharacteristic generosity.

We were once more overwhelmed with gratitude. Dear, dear Kunichin, he was being so kind. So understanding.

A few days later, Mother was sorting the washing to give to the dhobi-man.

"How on earth did you get into this state?" she asked, holding up our mud-caked clothes.

Beastly Kunichin, we thought, (forgetful that he had saved Peter's life,) he broke his promise. He just didn't bother, so Mother would find out.

"Oh," we said casually, "We went to the dam. . .It's all dried up, and we walked on the bottom and got a bit muddy,

Mother, engrossed in listing the washing, hardly listened to what we said and, to our relief, did not question us further, remaining unaware of how narrowly we had escaped disaster.

REPOSSESSING SUNNY JIM

"High o'er the fence leaps Sunny Jim," sang Peter, "Force is the stuff that raises him." As he sang he tossed the rag doll into the air and caught him again.

There were two Sunny Jims in the toy box. They had been made for us by Mother from printed kits, which she acquired while we were on leave in England, by sending coupons to the makers of what was one of the first breakfast cereals. They had cost sixpence each. Although they were superficially identical, Peter and I knew which was which, for mine had slightly more stuffing, and was plumper. In addition the two halves of his face had been sewn together so that they were slightly out of alignment, which gave his smile a certain wryness. Peter's Sunny Jim, on the other hand, had been printed a little darker, which with his slimmer form made him appear more dapper.

The dolls were the trade-mark of the cereal, representing a man with a white pigtail, a large nose and a monocle. The top of his head was a curious shape to indicate the billycock hat he wore. He held a packet of Force under one arm, which bore a picture of him on the outside, with another minute packet under his arm, too. And so on, ad infinitum. He was dressed in a red tailcoat, white breeches and spats. Although we had never seen anyone dressed in this manner, we were uncritical of his peculiar appearance, and were very attached to our halves of the twins.

The toy box in which they resided was not really a box at all, but a boat, whose misuse had been brought about by the inability of the village carpenter to follow Mother's description of a punt. The carpenter had never seen a punt. Probably he had never seen a boat either, except in pictures. There were coracles on the deeper pools of the river Periyar; crude craft made of buffalo hide stretched over a frame of branches, that were used for fishing, but locally there were no boats.

Our mother had requested a small flat-bottomed boat, which she thought would be fun and safe for us to use on the local stream. What the carpenter created was, it is true, a small flat-bottomed boat. It was about four feet long by fifteen inches wide, square at the stern, tapering in a graceful curve to the prow. It was painted white, inside and out, with the words, 'White Swan' in blue letters on one side. Peter and I were delighted.

Mother who was expecting something more on the lines of a simple box shape, was inclined to have doubts. Impatient as we were to try it out, we had to wait until the next morning, when the gardener carried it down to the stream for us. He was a good-looking young man, and very strong. We knew him only as Totemcurran, that being the Tamil word for gardener. His own name, a complicated Tamil one, we could not pronounce. He spoke no English, and Mother communicated with him by means of signs, or when that failed, through Kunichin acting as interpreter.

Dancing with excitement, we took off our clothes while he carefully lowered the 'White Swan' into the water, where it ran smoothly under the dappled shade of a grove of gum trees. Unlike its namesake, the 'White Swan' did not sail proudly on the water, but turned turtle and sank to the bottom. It was unfortunately quite the wrong shape; too narrow for a punt, lacking the keel that would have stabilised it as a boat.

Totemcurran righted it and tipped out the water, then signalled to us to get in. Holding the boat upright, he pushed us across the steam and back once or twice. Our mother had brought her Box Brownie camera with her in order to record the launching of this wonderful boat, so she took some snaps of us pretending to paddle ourselves along, with Totemcurran holding us upright, looking shy and handsome.

We soon tired of passively being pushed along, so Totemcurran shouldered the boat again and carried it back up the hill to the bungalow. There it was installed on the veranda outside our room, and served very well as a place to store our toys. However, now and then we would empty out the toys and pretend to sail it round the veranda.

We did not, in fact have a great many toys, by today's standards. I had a baby doll which I dressed in our outgrown baby clothes. They were rather too large for the doll and had to be held in place by a piece of ribbon tied round her waist. There were wooden hoops, and a pair of stilts, some rather battered skittles in the shape of soldiers and one or two wind-up tin cars, most of which had broken springs.

There was a large teddy bear that had belonged to our elder brother, who was now at school in England. The bear had lost both eyes, which had been replaced with brown trouser buttons. These gave him a peculiarly blank stupid look, which we disliked. Because of this we used him to vent our rage whenever we were unhappy or frustrated. As a result of our ill treatment Big Ted, as we called him, was almost bald, and his arms were rather loose.

Peter owned another bear, smaller and more appealing, called Little Ted. I owned a strange lumpish animal, meant to represent a dog couchant, having no legs, only little bumps for paws. Its once-stitched-down ears had come loose, and stood up above its head, so that those who were unfamiliar with it, thought, quite understandably that it was a toy rabbit. This dog, Fido, I took to bed with me at night. Like Big Ted, most of its hair had worn away.

Along with a box of bricks made of some sort of clay, the remains of our brother's Meccano set and, of course the Sunny Jim twins, that comprised the contents of the toy-box-boat.

It was not very often that we met other children, so we had to rely greatly on each other's company. There were very few European children in the district, while the local Indian children regarded us as strange, even bizarre. We were greeted whenever they saw us, by peals of laughter. By the time they were seven or eight years old, they were expected to take charge of their baby brothers and sisters so that their mothers could work.

The European children were usually sent away to school in England by the time they were seven. There were two little boys who we visited occasionally. Their mother, who was Dutch, kept a cow which she milked herself, and there were goats as well as ducks and chickens in a paddock behind their house. We enjoyed these visits but they were few and far between as they involved a long drive.

There was also a little girl called Betty who came to play sometimes. She was a pretty child, a bit younger than Peter, with fair hair arranged in ringlets. Since she was an only child we regarded her as 'spoilt'! One day she came to visit us with her mother. While our mothers sat talking in the sitting room, we were left to entertain her. We gave her turns on the swing and the see-saw, led her round the garden and played a game of hide-and-seek. We showed her how to suck honey from the flowers of a honeysuckle-like creeper we called tungipoo, and had races with her on our tricycles. All went smoothly and happily. Tea we ate alone on the nursery veranda, as had become usual when we had no guests. This was a treat for Betty, who was normally watched over by her ayah, left behind on this occasion.

After tea Betty sat down by the play-box boat to inspect the contents. Very soon she alighted on the Sunny Jims.

"What funny men!" she exclaimed. Peter and I began to chant the Sunny Jim rhyme in unison, and we all collapsed in giggles and began to invent some sort of game. Just then our mother and Mrs Shandon appeared, and stood regarding our game in amusement.

"I'm afraid it's time for Betty to go home." said Mrs Shandon." Oh, look. Isn't that amusing?" And she picked up Peter's Sunny Jim.

Mother explained how it had been acquired

"Oh, can I have one too?" Betty begged her mother, "I love him. He's so funny."

"Well," said Mrs Shandon, "I'm not sure. They don't sell Force here. We'll have to wait until we go home on leave."

That was when Mother, acting on the spur of the moment as she was sometimes apt to do, said: "Why don't we let Betty take one of them home with her?"

At that moment we were feeling that Betty was a sweet little girl. She had been co-operative all afternoon, and we had enjoyed her company. So we agreed that she should have one of the twins. It was Peter's that she chose.

"After all," Mother said, "you don't really want a doll, do you, darling? Aren't you a bit old for that?"

Pride caused Peter to agree, and he handed Sunny Jim over. We watched Betty hug him to her as she danced, ringlets bobbing, to where the car stood in the drive, and waved until she was out of sight.

The trouble was that though Sunny Jim may have looked like nothing more than an amusing rag doll to the Grown-ups, to us he had his own personality. We felt that he had feelings. To us it was as if we had handed over a puppy, or even a child.

"We'll see him again when we go to see Betty." We told each other, and I reassured Peter that Betty really did seem to like him, and after all she was a dear little girl, not spoilt at all.

"I'm sure she'll look after him." I said. Just the same we thought his twin looked a bit forlorn without him, his grin a trifle forced and wryer than ever.

It was a month or so before we made a return visit to see Betty. She was waiting for us on the veranda, dressed in her best dress, her ringlets carefully brushed, but beside herself with excitement. Her Ayah was fussing about her hair which was apparently less than perfectly arranged, and there was some crossness in the air because she would not stand still. Our mother was borne away by Mrs Shandon, and we were left in the Ayah's care. She clearly disapproved of us, knowing that we had no ayah ourselves, and no doubt suspected we might be too rough for her precious charge.

Betty was in such a state of excitement at our arrival that she was unable to think of any way to keep us amused. Instead she shouted, laughed uproariously, pulled faces and made us watch her dancing... something she could do with minimal ability. In fact she showed off and generally dominated the scene so that even her adoring Ayah became infuriated with her. We played Ring-o-roses once or twice, but Ayah thought she would spoil her dress when we fell down. Eventually tea was brought in, but Betty snatched the nicest cake, and spilt her milk.

After tea, bored, we began to look at her toys. She had cupboards full of beautiful fluffy stuffed toys, and dolls in elegant clothes. Ayah watched us closely and made sure we had washed our hands before we touched anything. Our patience was stretched to the limit.

Then we came across a wooden box containing a jumble of skipping ropes, pieces of puzzle and discarded toys. Peter and I began to rummage amongst them, trying to disentangle a rope to skip with. And there in the box we found Sunny Jim lying squashed and dusty under everything else.

Our irritation with Betty grew to resentment. We saw that she had had so much given to her that she had not valued her gift at all.

Sunny Jim stared pathetically at us through his monocle, his grin more forced than ever. We exchanged glances. We knew we had to do something. Peter picked him out of the box and brushed the dust off him.

Catching sight of the doll, Betty snatched him from Peter and flung him into the air, and let him fall to the floor.

"Oh, what a silly thing! " She said, kicking him aside, "Such a stupid looking man."

Politeness forbade that we should protest, but we were outraged. When Betty's attention was diverted elsewhere, Peter picked him up and pushed him under a cushion on a chair.

It was a long, trying afternoon. Peter and I, when we could escape Betty's demands for attention, whispered together and plotted.

At last it was time to go home. I picked up Sunny Jim, and held him so that he was between Peter and myself, and the skirt of my dress screened him from view. We edged towards the car, while the grown-ups were saying 'good-bye', and Betty was preoccupied with their attention. How were we to get him into the car without being seen?

As the grown-ups spoke to us, we passed Sunny Jim between us, keeping him behind us, and Peter managed to open the rear door slightly. As I leaned forward to kiss Mrs Shandon, Peter succeeded in sliding Sunny Jim into the back of the car and we climbed quickly in and sat on him. Our manners must have seemed distracted, but this was taken as shyness.

As we waved 'good-bye,' we breathed a sigh of relief that was tinged with guilt, because we knew we had robbed Betty. Mother drove us home, blissfully unaware of the refugee on the back seat.

"Did you enjoy yourselves?" she asked.

"Not much." said Peter, and I agreed.

"Betty's so spoilt. She just wants her own way all the time." I said.

"Well, she's an only child, of course." Mother said. "She is used to having all the attention."

"And she's got so many toys," we exclaimed.

Peter had taken Sunny Jim out and was pulling him back into shape. His grin seemed to us to show relief. His monocle winked at us.

"I'm never going to give her anything of mine again," Peter said.

"Nor am I." I said.

It was a long time before Betty visited us again. We took care to hide Peter's Sunny Jim before she came, but she caught sight of mine.

"Oh, I had one of those," she said.

"Yes, it was mine," said Peter.

"So it was. I don't know what happened to it. I haven't seen it for ages. It must be in the cupboard."

We maintained a discreet silence on the subject, but I caught Peter's eye. We both knew we had been right to repossess Sunny Jim. She hadn't even missed him.

FIRE-WALKERS AND A MISSIONARY

We lived in a remote place, surrounded only by villages whose inhabitants were extremely poor, relying for their existence on the tea plantations and their factories. For this reason there were, of course, few entertainments for the small scattering of Europeans apart from the Club. The nearest town, though it barely deserved that name, was Vandiperiyar, which consisted mainly of the Post Office, a small general store and the bazaar. Pigs, domesticated versions of wild boar, wallowed in the open drains that ran beside the road; chickens and pariah dogs wandered the street amongst the bullock-carts. There was, of course, no theatre or cinema. At that time there was no radio, television was unheard of, and the telephone had not yet reached beyond a few major cities. There was the telegraph at the Post Office but, apart from that, all the news we received from the outside world was by means of the Madras Mail, (a couple of days late,) and letters from England which took several weeks to reach us.

Fire-Walkers and a Missionary

The Club at Peermade was about half way between Arnakal and Vandiperiyar. Here the Europeans would gather to play tennis or bridge, and there would sometimes be dances. The adults met at dinner parties in each other's houses, and sometimes there were tennis parties at Arnakal.

Being unused to meeting our contemporaries, we were ill at ease in their company, and did not know what to say to them. However, we were seldom bored. We had a great deal of space and freedom, and invented our own games and our own imaginary world. The local children spoke no English, and were as shy as we were. They burst into giggles if we spoke to them. The girls of my age were expected to take care of their younger brothers and sisters, and usually had a baby straddling one immature hip.

Apart from the other planters and their wives, we had two regular callers at Arnakal.

One was a tallish, skinny old man, with matted grey hair, and milky-white eyes that stared blankly ahead. He would come every so often, leaning on a stick and led by a small boy. He was the Blind Beggar and would stand by the front steps, holding out a tin for our parents' contribution.

They would talk to him, asking how he was, and he would be given a few rupees and told to call in at the kitchen, where he and the boy would be given food. He wore an old jacket of Father's, which, in spite of Father being a very thin man, hung loosely on his shoulders. In wet weather he wore a piece of sacking to keep off the rain. Peter and I were nervous of him. We could not bring ourselves to look at those strange white eyes that seemed able to see invisible things.

The second regular caller came about once a month: the barber who came to cut everyone's hair. This was an operation Peter and I suffered with reluctance. Perched on a pile of cushions on a chair in our bathroom, swaddled in a towel, a pudding basin was placed firmly on our heads to ensure that the end result was even all round. Hair would fall in our eyes and get up our noses, making us sneeze. Peter, whose ears were inclined to stick out, was always afraid they would be nicked. The clippers were slightly blunt and dragged on the small hairs at the back of our necks. All of which increased our dislike of the proceedings.

The barber was a grave, respectful man, with hair and moustache as white as the blind man's. He had come regularly to ply his craft since our parents had first moved to Arnakal, after their honeymoon. He had learnt to shingle our mother's hair when that became the fashion.

My hair was always semi-shingled, which meant that it was trimmed to just above my ear lobes, and the back of my head cropped with the dreaded clippers. The front hair was scraped back from my face and firmly fastened with a bow or a slide. These always fell off during the day, and left me peering through my forelock like a Shetland pony. I yearned to be allowed a fringe and long hair.

"When I was a child," Mother used to tell us, "I had hair so long that I could sit on it."

I wished to be able to sit on my hair, but it was not to be. Every month the barber ensured that it was short and practical.

Occasionally some unusual thing happened. One day Francis and Kunichin came to tell us that a storyteller was visiting the village.

Fire-Walkers and a Missionary

"Come," said Francis. "I will take you. He says he will tell stories for you."

He and Kunichin gave us the impression that the man was someone special, and they both seemed very anxious that we should meet him. Francis was usually very strict with us, and Kunichin, too, seemed to disapprove of much that we got up to, so we were curious to meet this wonder. Of course, both the servants knew how much we enjoyed listening to stories.

It was a showery day, so we put on our raincoats and wellingtons, and followed Francis towards the village. On the way we came across a man in a parsee coat, squatting by the side of the road under a large black umbrella.

"Here he is," said Francis, with the air of presenting us with a special treat.

The man, on the other hand, appeared to be regarding us with a hostile stare. We were clearly not the audience he wanted. Perhaps he'd expected our parents, who, he hoped, would have paid him well.

"How are you?" he asked as we stood before him.

"Very well, thank you," said Peter, "Are you going to tell us a story?"

"Do you like to hear stories?" he asked.

"Oh, yes. We love them." I said.

"Love them? Love them? What is this then? How can you be loving a story? A story is not a thing to be loved. You can love God or your mother. You cannot love a story."

When he stopped speaking, Peter ventured: "Are you going to tell us a story?"

"No," the storyteller said, "I will not."

Francis pleaded with him. I told him our father would be pleased to give him money afterwards if he came to the bungalow, but in vain. The storyteller got to his feet and walked off under his black umbrella. We watched him disappear down the track.

Unaccustomed as we were to being rebuffed, we did not know what to make of him. We were used to being treated kindly. If Francis or Kunichin reprimanded us, even if we resented it, we usually knew it was deserved. As far as we knew we had done nothing to the storyteller, except misuse the word 'love'. It puzzled us, and the mystery was never solved.

It was a missionary who supplied us with a wonderful source of tales. Peter and I came across him talking to the servants on the kitchen veranda. They were all Christians, but he apparently thought they needed his message anyway. He seemed a friendly man, and began to ask us questions as we hopped about on some logs that were waiting to be cut up for firewood, until I stumbled and grazed my knee.

"Oh, I am so sorry!" the man called out to me.

"Why are you sorry?" Peter asked, "It wasn't your fault."

"Of course I am sorry. I am sorry your sister was hurt."

"It was my own fault." I said. "It wasn't anything to do with you. Anyway, it doesn't hurt much. You don't have to say sorry if you haven't done anything."

He still insisted on how deeply sorry he was, so we stopped discussing it. We knew that my graze meant nothing to him, since he was a stranger to us.

Fire-Walkers and a Missionary

He stayed talking to us for a bit, telling us about God's love, and how small accidents, like my falling off the log could change someone's whole life. We liked him, but thought he was simple minded.

He had a small case with him filled with tracts and booklets from which, when he left, he extracted a pamphlet, which he gave to us. It was full of unlikely stories of terrible tragedies and disasters caused by such small, unexpected mishaps as a driver sneezing, or getting a grit in his eye at the wrong moment. The final paragraph of each story drew a moral conclusion. Peter and I loved it. I read and re-read it. It had the same sort of attraction as the rhymes in 'Strewel Peter', (Shock-headed Peter,) which we knew so well. Augustus who would not eat his soup, and starved to death within a week, and Harriet and the matches which caused her to burn to death. We found the missionary's book just as preposterous. After the disillusioning encounter with the storyteller, the missionary left us with a rich source of fantasy. He did not, however return.

There was one event that was especially memorable. Our nearest neighbour was the junior assistant-manager, Mr Wilshaw. He lived a quarter of a mile distant, in the Little Bungalow, which was just visible above the cedar avenue across the valley from our house. We had lived there for a time before we went on leave, when Mr Wilshaw's predecessor had left, and the 'Old Bungalow ' was being knocked down and rebuilt. Now and then, in want of something to do, Peter and I would call in on Mr Wilshaw to say hello. Sometimes he would be entertaining guests, and we would hang about, not quite knowing how to leave. We were usually given lemonade, and the

The Tea Planter's Children

guests would laugh at our replies to their questions, but then ignore us. They were always strangers to us, Anglo-Indians like Mr Wilshaw, and livelier and more colourful than the local white residents.

One day we found that he was being entertained by a troupe of firewalkers and acrobats. He was sitting alone on his veranda waiting for their performance to begin, and suggested that we might as well stay and watch. Even at seven or eight, we were intrigued that he had commanded this entertainment just for himself.

Although we had seen snake charmers, we had never before seen the feats that were performed that afternoon. A fire-eater thrust burning brands into his mouth and breathed out flames like dragon's breath. Braziers of red-hot charcoal smouldered on the front drive, from which the performers, a rather shabby troupe of men and small boys, fuelled their primitive equipment. The boys, holding iron rods from which hung small baskets of glowing embers, whirled them round their heads and turned somersaults. All the tricks involved fire in some form. The men and boys formed themselves into pyramids, holding flaming brands, whirled, somersaulted and breathed fire.

There were often long pauses between acts, while the braziers were restoked. Mr Wilshaw seemed dissatisfied with whatever they did, though Peter and I were impressed. The head of the troupe, a smallish, stocky man in a sweat-stained shirt, his dhoti drawn up between his legs, as is the Indian custom when engaged in anything strenuous, made low salaams of apology to Mr Wilshaw. The perspiration was dripping from his face although it was late afternoon and the air was cooling.

Fire-Walkers and a Missionary

"What about the firewalking you told me you would do?" Mr Wilshaw demanded ungratefully.

"Yes, sahib, later. Later. We will do, sahib. Please be waiting, sahib."

So the small boys whirled and somersaulted with their firebrands. It was a brave and desperate performance, but lacked polish.

As a final gesture the contents of the charcoal braziers were strewn across the drive and raked to an even bed. They cooled to ashy black while this was done. Then first one and then another of the troupe, looking anxious as if they were unused to performing this particular feat, launched themselves barefoot across the coals, taking long, rapid strides. They stood together in a row, put their hands together and bowed low before us. The leader came over to Mr Wilshaw. "I don't think much of that. The fire was out before you crossed it. I'm not paying you for that." Mr Wilshaw said.

The leader looked distressed and began to argue, waving his hands about. The troupe stood in a cross, depressed huddle, muttering to each other.

"I've seen better in Madras," Mr Wilshaw went on, "And for less money than you're asking."

At that point we heard the gong sounding from our bungalow and knew that it was time for our supper. We were relieved to have an excuse to go, for it looked as though it was going to be a long argument. We never heard whether the braziers were refilled and relighted and strewn again, or whether the troupe settled for less money. Either way they were bound to lose.

These events were rare and therefore assumed an importance in our lives and we discussed them long afterwards. They became part of our legends.

LUNCHING WITH FATHER

We regarded Father with awe. Tall and thin, and plagued with duodenal ulcers, he had a loud voice, and his years in the Army during the Boer War and the Great War, as our parents referred to it, gave him a peremptory manner and a sarcastic wit. In spite of this we admired and respected him because, although he demanded high standards of behaviour from us, he also had a softer, gentler side. We did not see him very much during the day, naturally, as he was busy with estate business, but in the evening, after we had had our bath and supper, we would spend half-an-hour or so with him, playing rough-and-tumble games, as he sprawled in his armchair by the log fire that was usually lighted in the cool of the evening. We would tell him of things we had learnt during the morning lessons, or had discovered during the day, and he would invent wonderful stories for us.

Our meals were eaten separately from our parents at a child-sized table with child-sized chairs on the nursery veranda. Mother, after the departure of the New Ayah, sat with us in a bent-wood rocking chair and read to us from Grimm's Fairy tales, Aesop's Fables, Christopher Robin or some other children's stories. She also taught us how to use our cutlery, eat with our mouths shut, not to slurp our soup and the necessary table manners.

After lunch we would go for our afternoon rest with a boiled sweet to suck, (one sweet a day!) while she joined Father for their own meal.

One day Mother said: "How would you like to have your pudding with Daddy and me? I think you're old enough to join us, but of course you must remember to behave well or Daddy won't want you to eat with us."

From that time we began to take our dessert in the dining room with our parents. Sitting up at the table with its crisp white cloth and starched napkins, polished silver plate cutlery and serving dishes while waited on by Francis or Kunichin, was an over-awing experience. Flattered to be regarded as fit for grown-up company, we sat, legs dangling, raised by means of cushions or thick books to enable us to see over the table, and tried to eat our rice pudding as politely as we could.

Father's comments were usually half humorous, and had we been the soldiers he had once served with, we might have been amused instead of cringing.

"Don't swallow your spoon, Eve!" he roared. "There's no need to put the whole thing into your mouth. Now you're doing it again. Stop it, do you hear?"

I cowered over my plate as I tried to amend my use of the spoon.

"We'll have to tie the spoon to the table leg," he went on, "We can't afford to have you swallowing the cutlery. I knew a little girl once, who was just like you. She kept swallowing her spoons. You could hear them rattle when she walked. Her mummy and daddy couldn't think what

Lunching with Father

to do. It would be very expensive to keep operating on her to get the spoons back, but they were running short of them. Besides, all that clinking wherever she went was annoying. So they tied a piece of string to the handle," Father was chuckling as he spoke, "and fastened the other end to the table leg. After that, if the spoon went down, they could jerk it back again. We'll have to do something like that for you, won't we?"

He looked at me as he laughed at his own fantasy, while I giggled nervously and stared down at my milk pudding.

Later we were promoted to eating the whole of our midday meal with our parents. Their intention was to ensure that we knew how to behave in adult society and learned how to converse, as well as to practise our table manners. Father, whose ulcer made him impatient, would reprimand our lapses and tell us improbable stories about what became of children who persisted in eating with their mouths open or gulped their drinks. On his bad days, when his ulcers were giving him a lot of pain, he could be exceedingly intolerant of even minor lapses, which increased our nervousness of him.

There came a day when Mother was visiting her friend, Madge Cargil, at Munjamully.

"How is Mac?" Madge asked as they set out on a walk together.

"I'm afraid he's been having a bad time lately, poor dear, " said Mother, "but he should soon be feeling better, because the wretched ulcer has burst, and he's passing a lot of blood, getting rid of the horrid thing."

Madge, seeing, as Mother obviously did not, the significance of this remark, made her return with her to the house immediately to find her husband, Jim. When he heard the news he sent for Mr Gowan, Father's assistant, and persuaded him to telegraph to the company head office, reporting Father's illness, also to Dr Somervell at Vallore, asking him to come at once, and be prepared to operate.

A brilliant surgeon, Dr Somervell was also a noted mountaineer who had accompanied Mallory on his expeditions to Everest.

Mr Gowan was reluctant to comply, fearing Father's reaction to his interference, but was finally persuaded of the urgency of the situation. Then the Cargils set about helping Mother to get everything ready for the doctor's arrival. Peter and I were taken to stay at Munjamully, blissfully unaware of the drama that was taking place.

Later that day, Father felt a little better, and announced that he was not going to be fussed over by any doctors, and sent Mother to drive to the Post Office to dispatch a cable stopping the doctor and his nurse. As luck would have it, Jim Cargil met her as she was on her way and with great difficulty managed to prevent her from carrying out her errand.

Dr Somervell arrived early next day, after travelling all night. He appeared flushed and wild eyed, but saw at once how serious Father's condition was, so prepared everything as quickly as he could.

Father's operation was carried out with a spinal anaesthetic, (a technique that Dr Somervell had developed), on the dining table, which was placed on the veranda, for the sake of maximum light. Nine inches of his small intestine was removed. It was touch and go. Any further delay would almost certainly have been fatal.

Afterwards it was discovered that Dr Somervell was himself ill, and running a high temperature. He gave strict orders that Father should be given nothing but fluids for the next few days, and then he retired to the spare bedroom to sleep. However, later that evening he was woken by the smell of toasting cheese, and discovered that Father had persuaded Mother that that was what he craved, so she had gone to the kitchen to make it for him! Eating it could have killed him!

Next morning the doctor left, but later that day Mother sent an urgent message to Munjamully, asking Jim Cargil to come as soon as he could. He arrived to find that Father was having an attack of hiccups, which nothing seemed to remedy. He was in agony, and Mother was afraid to leave his bedside in case he got up and did something desperate. Jim sat with him all day and late into the night, when at last the hiccups left him and he fell asleep.

Through all this, Peter and I were being kept busy and entertained and in ignorance by Aunt Madge, and were quite unaware of the seriousness of Father's condition, as it was deemed unsuitable for us children to be involved. Aunt Madge had the ability to recite the Just-So stories by heart, which greatly endeared her to us, and she knew the names and calls of most of the wild birds that inhabited the nearby jungle, so we were most happy to be her guests.

As soon as Father was judged to be on the road to recovery, we returned home to find him propped up in bed with the half-dozen pillows with which he habitually slept, looking extremely pale and fragile.

After the incident with the toasted cheese, Mother was strict with Father's diet, and whatever we had for lunch, Father was given boiled chicken, or, when it was available, boiled or steamed fish. After a few weeks, he rebelled and sent his plate back to the kitchen, while he stated forcefully that he never wanted to eat blasted boiled chicken again for the rest of his life !

A month or so after his operation, it was decided that Father would benefit from a voyage to Australia, where one or two of his old friends had settled. Being a rather unsociable man, and still feeling far from fit, he did not much enjoy the life on board ship, but it did him good and he returned, glad to be home , and looking well again.

Our awe of Father was shared, naturally, by the servants, who had great respect for him. They were also touchingly loyal to him. On one occasion there was an epidemic of flu' which laid most of the staff low. Replacements were found, but they were inefficient and unreliable. One morning our parents woke to find that the early morning tea had failed to materialise, but there was the sound of wood being chopped outside.

On investigation, Kunichin, aged about twelve at the time, was discovered wielding an axe almost as large as himself, trying to cut wood for the stove in order to make the tea. Francis, having struggled to keep going, although stricken with the flu', had finally had to give in as he too ill to get up, and was later found to have developed pleurisy.

Some months after Father returned from Australia, he was about to leave the house to walk to a distant part

Lunching with Father

of the estate where he wanted to check a nursery that was being pruned, when Francis approached him.

"Excuse please, Sahib." He said," Here is coolie want ask Sahib, has Sahib work he can do ?"

We saw a small man with an untidily wound turban and a drooping moustache, standing on the front drive. As Father walked over to speak to him, the man cowered before him, bowing low and reaching out with his hands to touch Father's shoes.

After listening to his pleas for a few moments, he looked exasperated. We heard him say: "Dammit, I sacked you only last month because you do not work well. What do you mean by coming back again ? Surely you don't expect me to give you another job, after that ? You were utterly incompetent."

The man began to beg, hands placed together as he bowed low, ready to throw himself at Father's feet.

Father turned and began to walk away, saying loudly over his shoulder: "Oh, very well then. You can try. I'll give you one more chance. Be here tomorrow morning. Francis, you must show him what to do."

He told us that he had taken the man on out of pity as his personal servant to look after his clothes, fill his bath, and fetch his shaving water. He was called Muthu, like the cook, but he was as unlike the cook as can be imagined. Somehow he always looked untidy, his clothes too big for him. Even his dhoti seemed to swamp his skinny figure. He spoke almost no English and was terrified of Father. He must have been truly desperate to ask him for work.

His reputation for incompetence was confirmed by his inability to knock at the dressing room door before entering. He would fling the door open only to be greeted by a roar from Father, caught in a state of disrobement or in the process of using the lavatory. Time and again he would emerge from the encounter trembling and tearful, only to burst in again on the next occasion.

Finally, after Father had become almost apoplectic with frustration at his inability to understand that he must knock and wait until told to "Come in", Muthu worked out a solution. He would arrive at the dressing room door, which led out of the passage between the dining room and the kitchen. There he would wait until he thought no one was watching, and then peer through the keyhole to see if Father was in the room. If he were, Muttu would go away and return later. If no one were in view, he would rap on the door and go in. This system ensured that Father never knew how long he would have to wait for his bath or shaving water, and that it was usually luke-warm by the time it was delivered.

For some reason, Father bore with Muthu for several months before he found him a menial task on the plantation, and we no longer glimpsed the untidy form crouched by the dressing room door, his eye glued to the keyhole.

After his operation Father began to be concerned about my health, suspecting that like him, I might be prone to ulcers. He insisted that I swallow a teaspoonful of bicarbonate in a wine glass of water after lunch every day. I was also, because of my dislike of milk, made to eat a daily slice of toast and cottage cheese. I eventually grew to be able to tolerate both these dietary impositions.

"You're walking like a chicken!" he would bark at me, as I tried to pass him unobserved, "Hold your head up! Put your shoulders back!"

This lead to my receiving an exercise period every morning before breakfast. I had to report to his dressing room for drill. He taught me to bend, stretch, swing my arms, do deep breathing and march round the room with a book balanced on my head.

Peter and I were both in awe of Father, with his loud voice and sarcastic tongue. However, while these drill sessions lasted I learnt to be less afraid of him. Alone with me, he was gentler in his approach and his comments were less crushing.

Just the same, lunch with Father was an experience to be endured rather than enjoyed, though the stories he told us before we went to bed, were always something we looked forward to with pleasure as then he would be relaxed and not concerned with trying to improve us.

WAKING FROM DREAMS

I woke to find my pillow damp with tears. I had been dreaming, as I sometimes did, that I was walking beside Old Ayah, reaching up to hold her hand, with a sense of happiness because she had come back again. As usual, when consciousness returned, I remembered that she had not come back and there was only the remotest chance that we would ever see her again. She had moved on to look after another family when we all went Home on leave, and on our return her place was taken by the new Ayah, entirely different in character and much disliked by Peter and myself. In less than a year this new Ayah was, to our relief, dismissed and not replaced.

Old Ayah, as we always referred to her, had looked after us all from the day we were born until our departure on that leave. Saying 'Goodbye' to her, we children felt bereft. Peter and I were too young to be fully conscious that the parting was to be permanent, but for Ann who was to be left behind in England, it was a kind of amputation. Robert had already gone, taken to England to start school by family friends, and had experienced the sense of loss that so many colonial children suffered on

Waking from Dreams

leaving Ayah and the family to face the world on his own at the age of eight.

Ayah had come to Arnakal before Robert's birth, a quiet, patient woman whose own daughters had grown up and married. The lobes of her ears hung down to her shoulders under the weight of her gold earrings. This was the custom among Indian women, who did not trust Banks and believed that their savings, converted into gold, could not easily be stolen from their ears. Unfortunately, sometimes, ruthless thieves did not hesitate to cut off the lobes to steal the gold.

Her habit, which she had in common with Francis, of chewing betelnut stained her teeth and gums red, and gave a peculiar smell to her breath. She looked older than her years after the loss of most of her teeth through a gum infection. In later years it was a lasting regret on Mother's part that she did not pay for her to be fitted with false teeth.

From time to time her daughters used to visit her and sit with her in her sparsely furnished room in the servants' quarters, nursing their babies and swapping gossip for advice. Once when Ayah had taken me there with her, probably soon after Peter was born, her daughter was feeding her baby and I must have shown a desire to suckle, too.

Ayah had laughed, and said "Go on, let her try." So her daughter picked me up and gave me her breast. Perhaps their laughter embarrassed me, or perhaps the milk had a taint of the spicy food she ate. Whatever it was, I did not like it, and from then on took a dislike to milk.

One day, when I was about three or four years old, one of her daughters brought her little girl with her, a child a little younger than I was. It had evidently been decided that it was time for her ears to be pierced.

Our parents were out and Ayah was mending our clothes while she looked after us. She selected a large needle from the sewing basket, and found a matchstick, then went out to where her daughter was waiting with the little girl.

I heard the child's screams, and Ayah and her daughter's voices soothing and consoling her. When Ayah returned to put away the needle, the little girl followed her, still sniffling, her cheeks wet with tears, and each of her earlobes skewered with half a match: the first step towards her first earrings, and her first savings towards her dowry. I was very thankful that it would not be necessary for me to undergo such an ordeal.

Most of my memories of Ayah were happier. She was a constant presence in her white sari, always watching over us, comforting us when we fell over, scolding us when we were wilful, quietly seated mending our clothes with unbelievably small stitches as we played. In my recurring dreams she would be taking me for a walk with the motley collection of dogs which we owned at that time, holding my hand and telling me stories. Whether they were tales with a moral pointing out what accidents might befall me if I failed to heed her warnings, or fairy tales that differed from the ones our mother read to us, but bore many similarities, I was an avid listener.

She called us her 'Golden Babies', and longed to become white. Sometimes when she came with us to the stream where we paddled, we noticed her scrubbing her legs and feet with sand.

"What are you doing, Ayah?" we asked.

"I want to make my skin white like yours." she said, serious and regretful.

The New Ayah, engaged to take care of Peter and me on our return from leave, was everything Old Ayah was not. A young woman, she came to earn money to provide for her children since her husband was in debt. No doubt she missed her children and resented our easy lives, but she did not know how to control us without recourse to threats and bribes.

"My husband will bring you a rickshaw full of rubies." She used to promise me. "When he comes he will bring you pearls and diamonds and golden bangles."

For some reason she did not like Peter, and made that plain every day. We did not understand why she disliked him, but her nastiness to him, the pinches she gave him, and her habit of comparing him unfavourably to me, earned our hatred of her. Where Old Ayah could be firm but kind, she was spiteful and threatened us with vile punishments if we disobeyed her.

"I will pinch your legs until there is no skin left." She told four year old Peter.

On occasions when she bathed us and Peter got soap in his eyes, if he cried out "Soap!" she was likely to add another spongeful, pretending that she thought he had been calling for more.

I too got a share of pinches and menaces, but for some reason she preferred me, so coaxed me to co-operate with her ridiculous bribes that I knew were fantasies. Why was she working for us if her husband was so rich? I regarded her as a liar.

In the end we were rescued by chance. Mother was in a room overlooking our veranda with the window ajar.

She overheard New Ayah threatening Peter, who would not eat his lunch, with one of her bizarre tortures.

It was a rule of Mother's that children must never be threatened unless that threat could be carried out promptly if they disobeyed. On hearing New Ayah's grotesque threats, she dismissed her at once.

Peter and I felt a huge sense of relief at her departure, though we wondered who would replace her. It was then that it was decided that we were old enough to do without an ayah, that Mother, with help from Kunichin, could very well look after us herself. I did not dream of New Ayah, even in nightmares, though it is possible that Peter did.

One day Kunichin came to fetch us from where we were playing, with a message from Mother.

"Come quickly," he said," There is someone to see you."

Mystified, we ran to the front of the bungalow where we saw Mother standing near the front steps talking to a small woman in a white sari.

"Look who's here," she said, smiling. "You remember who this is, don't you?"

"Ayah?" I guessed shyly. Peter and I were both tongue-tied. Two or even three years had passed since we had last seen her, and in that time she seemed to have dwindled and become unfamiliar. She laughed as she greeted us, but she too was affected by how we had altered from the children she remembered.

I did not know how to tell her how much I had missed her. She had become a stranger, even her voice seemed quieter, more hesitant, unfamiliar. She seemed so small, so old, with her grey hair and her glasses. Embarrassed,

Waking from Dreams

I stood, shifting from foot to foot, smiling shyly. Peter clung to Mother's hand and stared in silence at this little brown woman with her toothless smile, and her metal framed spectacles.

She explained that she was visiting her daughters, and had wanted to see us again, the family she had worked for and been loved by for ten years. Mother asked her if she was still with the family she had gone to after leaving us.

Yes, the madam was very kind to her, and had paid for her to get her glasses, as she had found it hard to see to sew. She was very grateful that Mother had found her such a good family to work for.

It was clear that she was as shy of us as we were of her, for we were no longer the three year old and five year old children she had so sadly bidden 'Goodbye'.

Mother found some way to let us go, and I ran off in guilty relief. I felt I had betrayed the dream I had held to all that time, and was ashamed that I was unable to talk to this person I had loved and had so much longed to see again. I did not understand why I felt so uncomfortable.

Afterwards, my dream rarely came back to me, and when it did, I no longer shed tears on waking. I remembered the awkwardness of that meeting, and understood a little that we had all changed. Time had made an unbridgeable gap between the people we had been and the people we had become. Although I resented having to relinquish the dream of what had been, I knew I could never return there, to the land of the past, which now included that reunion, nor could I ever change any part of it.

GARDENS OF REMEMBRANCE

Because the bungalow at Arnakal was situated on a hillside, the land had been made level by terracing to form the garden, which extended all the way round the house. The upper terraces were laid out with lawns and flower beds, while the lower levels were shady with trees and flowering shrubs, and were reached down stone steps beneath pergolas of roses and creepers. Peter and I were allotted a small corner of the garden to cultivate.

As with most children's gardens, our plot was an unpromising patch, situated near the garage, where a rose apple tree overhung a corner of the drive. We used to dig here with our mother's trowel. Peter was not much interested in growing plants, but I had planted some clumps of lilies and cannas, the thinnings from the main garden, and now and then the remains of packets of seeds. I always hoped that one day they would produce a blaze of flowers, but the situation was too shady, the soil leached dry by the roots of the rose apple. All they ever produced were leaves.

Gardens of Remembrance

It was while I was digging amongst the plants that I unearthed a huge grub. We decided that it was a cockchafer larva. About two inches long, creamy white with a head the colour of marigolds, many legs and a fat, slightly glossy body. To us it had a sort of beauty.

Always encouraged, as we were, to take an interest in the insects and animals that abounded there, we thought we would like to keep the grub and watch as it turned into a cockchafer. The question was, how?

It was slow moving, and since I had found it underground, we decided to keep it in a flowerpot full of earth. Every day or so we unearthed it again to see how it was faring.

After a short time it began to look less pretty. Its creamy body seemed to be fading to a sickly greenish grey, and had lost its sheen. It looked weak and slightly shrivelled. It began to disgust us, part of our disgust being compounded with guilt that we were responsible for its decline. We did not know how to make it well again, and saw that it was probable that it was dying.

Having had instilled into us the principle that if a creature was mortally ill or injured, we were obliged to end its suffering as quickly and mercifully as possible, the only way we could see to deal with the cockchafer larva, would be to stamp on it, but neither of us could bring ourselves to do that. We could visualise the result. Besides we could no longer bear to touch it. So we made a hole and buried it, hoping that, since we had found it underground, it might recover there. We were pretty sure that it would not and our garden lost its attraction for some time.

However, it was another grave that was to be my first success in my attempts to make a garden.

Beside the dogs and cats and other occasional more exotic pets we acquired, there was a permanent collection of chickens, ducks and turkeys at the back of the house. They were for use as required for the table, and replenished by fresh stock bought in the bazaar at Vandiperyar. They were carried home on the postman's bicycle, upside down with their legs tied together.

At least that was how the hens and turkeys travelled. The ducks, whose legs were fragile, were carried by the neck! I'm not sure how they survived this treatment, but on arrival they settled in quite happily.

One day Peter and I were in the yard behind the kitchen when we caught sight of an exceptionally beautiful bird amongst the hens. It was a young cock, with a scarlet comb like a crown, and golden feathers round his neck. His back and breast were chestnut red, his wings peacock green, as were the fluttering plumes of his tail. He was magnificent.

Peter and I rushed to fetch our mother, who shared our admiration, and we extracted, without difficulty a promise that he would not be served up for lunch !

So he survived to rule the chickens and strut among the more ordinary fowls. We made a great fuss of him, and allowed him to wander into the main garden and scratch where he liked. We used to save our crusts and scraps of food for him. We called him Chanticlere.

After a while, we began to notice that Chanticlere was no longer strutting about, boastfully crowing. He did not seem interested in the scraps we brought him and allowed the other birds to snatch them. He sat listlessly

Gardens of Remembrance

in a corner, his magnificent crown purplish and inclined to flop sideways.

We called Mother to look at him. She went to consult 'The Children's Encyclopaedia', our favourite source of reference, to learn what she could about the diseases of poultry.

"It must be croup," she told us.

We made him a bed in a box of straw to keep him warm. Mother tried to dose him with drops of brandy, but he struggled hard when we tried to open his beak, and most of it spilt. He shook his head, then closed his yellow eyes, and looked more miserable than ever. In the morning he was dead.

We wept for him, for he had been so proud and so beautiful. To comfort us, Mother suggested that we have a funeral.

"You could bury him in the kitchen garden." She suggested, when we refused to make the grave in our garden, because of the cockchafer larva buried there.

The ground was too hard for us to manage a deep enough hole, but Totemcuran, the gardener saw us struggling and came to our rescue.

As he spoke no English, he was always silent in our presence, and we were a little in awe of him, but we were touched by the care he took to make the hole deep enough to take poor Chanticlere's cardboard coffin. Clutching our bunches of funeral flowers, we stood watching him, as he put back half the earth from the grave, then signalling to us to wait, walked away to where the plantains and guavas grew. There he dug up a plantain sapling which he replanted on the grave. As he replaced the rest of the soil, he trod it down firmly round the plantain roots and shaped the grave round the palm into a small mound, on which we laid our flowers.

We stood back to admire it, and then turned to Totemcuran, who smiled in silence as we expressed our gratitude for his thoughtfulness.

From then on he included the palm when he watered the vegetable garden, and no doubt, that was why it flourished.

Later, when our mother pruned the roses, I collected some of the prunings and stuck two into the soil of the grave. To my delight they took root and in time flowered abundantly. I had also planted a few nasturtium seeds. They too, germinated, and spread across the mound, hanging down the sides until, under the plantain and the roses, Chanticlere's grave was garlanded with their round leaves and orange flowers.

I used to go down there frequently to weed and water the plants on what had become a shrine. It was the first success I had had at gardening, and it filled me with pride.

In the other garden, under the rose apple tree, where the lilies and cannas continued to produce nothing but leaves, the tomb of the cockchafer larva lay neglected.

UNSUITABLE PETS

One morning just before Easter, the year we returned from leave, Peter was left with the new Ayah, whilst Mother took me with her to visit the Rice Merchant, to pay our bill and order fresh supplies for the household.

The Rice Merchant was the wealthiest Indian in the District, probably wealthier than most of the Europeans, if the truth be known. We found him in the big corrugated iron building on the Munjamully road that was his warehouse. There were hessian sacks stacked high round the walls, and by the doorway other sacks, the tops rolled back, displayed their contents. Orange lentils, yellow and green dried peas, brown unpolished rice, and rice that was pearly white. It smelt of rice and tobacco.

The Rice Merchant was a plump, affable man, with a fine moustache. He was known for his generous gifts, most of which had to be tactfully returned, lest they were taken to be bribes. At each of our births he had given us twenty gold sovereigns, and every Christmas he brought us lavish presents. Those of lesser value were accepted graciously.

That day he was welcoming and effusive as ever, and after exchanging greetings with my mother, turned to me and asked whether I was looking forward to Easter.

"Is the Easter rabbit coming to bring you Easter eggs?" he asked.

"We haven't got a rabbit now." I replied, not understanding the allusion, for I had not been told the legend.

"Haven't you got a rabbit? Really? Oh, that is too bad." he said, sympathetically. "Perhaps you don't like rabbits then?"

I said that, yes, indeed I did. Of course I did, but the rabbits we had once had all died.

"That is very sad. You really should have a rabbit for Easter." He turned to Mother. "Madam, will you allow me to give the little missie a rabbit? I have one that I know she will like. May I give it to your daughter for an Easter present?"

I heard my mother agree, and they went on to discuss the account and the supplies that were needed. He enquired solicitously after my father and siblings, as they completed their business talk, then we returned home. I did not believe that he really was going to give me a rabbit. I expected that he would forget.

A few days later, however, a boy arrived holding a bundle of soft white fur. It was a very beautiful white angora rabbit, the most beautiful pet I had ever had. I had envisaged an ordinary black and white or brown rabbit, such as we had had at the Old Bungalow, nothing as glamorous as this. I was beside myself with delight.

A hutch was hastily constructed from an old commode, with wire-netting tacked across the hole in the seat. It was

Unsuitable Pets

placed on its side so the rabbit, which I had named Easter, could look out, and I could see it. Peter and I spent a long time stroking it and admiring it before it was put into the hutch which was placed on the floor of the veranda just outside our bedroom. Digger tried to take an interest too, but we did not trust him and shooed him away.

It was Easter next day. We went to bed in a high state of excitement at not just the expectation of coloured eggs for breakfast, and perhaps a chocolate or sugar egg from our father, but the knowledge that there existed, just outside our room, this new and fabulous pet.

That morning I awoke early, climbed out of bed through my mosquito net and went straight on to the veranda to see Easter. At first I did not understand what had happened. The hutch was empty, the wire netting across the front crumpled inwards. I thought Easter must have escaped, and began to hunt round the veranda for the bundle of white fluff that had just become my most prized possession.

Then, glancing across the flowerbed that edged the veranda to the lawn beyond, a horrific scene met my eyes. The grass, still wet with dew, was strewn with fragments of scarlet flesh and white fur. At first I was unable to grasp what I was seeing, until I recognised a long pinky-white ear. On the far side of this carnage, the black dog, Digger was crouched, tearing at a large portion of what had so recently been Easter, my beautiful rabbit.

As I understood that this was no nightmare, but the slaughter of my adored pet, I began to scream. At the sound, Peter climbed out of his cot and, seeing what had happened, began to scream too. Alarmed by our shrieks, Mother, in her kimono, came running out of her bedroom and rushed over to Digger. He tried to slink away, but his greed was too great, and as he snatched another mouthful of poor Easter, she caught him, slapped him hard, and dragged him away to be tied up.

I do not know who removed the ghastly remains of my beloved rabbit. I was taken sobbing, back into the house by Ayah, to be comforted and appeased.

It was a long time before I was able to forgive Digger.

That was the first of many small tragedies amongst our pets, and the most horrific.

It was not long after this that Francis and Kunichin, attempting to compensate me for the loss of Easter, brought a new animal to show me: a young leveret. The little hare did not have the glamorous looks of the angora rabbit, but it was an attractive rusty brown little creature with long ears and large dark eyes. It was still wild, and very nervous, but of course, it at once became the centre of my affections.

The commode-hutch was reinstated, but this time, placed on a cupboard, with the wire firmly secured across the opening, so there could be no chance of Digger helping himself to another feast.

A week later, the servants brought a second leveret, which they gave to Peter. It was calmer and a little smaller than mine. We called them 'Run-Run' and 'Bun-Bun'. Taken from the wild, as they had been, they remained wild, and when we took them out of the hutch to exercise them and to play with them, they always tried to bolt. At first, being small and young, we could recapture them fairly easily, but as they grew it became increasingly hard, so that we soon realised that they would have to have more space in which to live. With this in mind a wire-netting run was constructed in a part of the lower garden.

Here we thought they would enjoy nibbling the grass, which had been allowed to grow long. The enclosure was about four feet by two, the wire supported by bamboo stakes. We took Bun-Bun first, as the larger, wilder, and harder to catch of the two when played with on the veranda, and therefore most in need of a run.

Having first ensured that Digger was safely tied up, we placed her inside the enclosure. Before we had time to straighten up, she took off, and leapt full-tilt down the run, crashing into the netting at the end. Before any of us could stop her, she turned and sprang back the other way, to crash once more against the wire. By now her nose was bleeding, and her terror and panic was increasing. It was difficult to catch her, as she leapt and dodged around the run, crashing into the wire again and again, but finally we succeeded, and bore her, terrified and struggling, back to the hutch.

Since Run-Run was smaller, and tamer, we decided to see if he, at least, would enjoy the greater freedom of the run, but the results were the same, except that, being prepared for what could happen, we recaptured him more quickly.

There was only one conclusion to draw, namely that they were too wild to keep as pets, so we must free them as soon as possible.

Sadly, we took them up to the Green Hill, a favourite place well away from any houses, where hares were sometimes seen, and they would be unlikely to be caught by dogs. They raced away from us, jinxing in and out of the clumps of citronella grass, until they were lost to view.

Peter and I cherished the vain hope that one day they would see us and come back to let us pet them again, so always looked for them on our walks to the Green Hill. But we never saw them again.

Once or twice Kunichin caught baby bulbuls for me, but Mother always insisted that they were released at once.

"You can't keep birds in a cage," she would tell me, "It's so cruel. Birds need to be able to fly."

The Sweeper-woman's son was the source of my next attempt to keep unusual pets. He was a shy little boy, about a year younger than I was, who spoke no English. He came to the house with his mother each day while she swept the floors and cleaned the lavatories silently, with a kind of patient dignity.

One day, when he saw me, he grinned at me and showed me that he had something clasped between his hands. At first I did not know what he was holding, but on close inspection, I saw that it was a nest of baby rats.

"Give them to me, please." I said, but he giggled nervously and shook his head. I tried to argue with him, but he only continued to grin and shake his head.

Determined to see them, I wrestled with him until he let go of them. I felt guilty about it, and knew that I was in the wrong, for rats were a major pest and the coolies were rewarded for killing them. Every morning they would line up outside the Estate Office below the bungalow with either the bodies or the tails of dead rats and be paid a few pice for each one.

Unsuitable Pets

There were sixteen rats in the nest; eight were still hairless, pink and blind; eight had fur, and were beginning to open their eyes. To me they were helpless, baby creatures that I wanted to take care of and keep as pets.

I told him that he must ask our father to pay him. The Sweeper-woman and her son were Untouchables, and I was not sure that I should have grappled hold of him to rescue the rats. I thought I might have broken a taboo, but I was determined that these, to my eyes, sweet little creatures should not be killed.

I tried to feed them by soaking pieces of cotton wood in milk and encouraging them to suck, but the hairless ratlets began to die fairly soon, and, despite my protests, they were taken from me.

One of the Company Agents was staying with us at the time. He had brought with him his daughter, a young woman in her twenties. It was Susan who had insisted that I was being cruel in trying to rear such young creatures, and ordered a basin of water to be brought. She drowned them then and there. I watched their struggles in anguish. Probably their death took only seconds, but they seemed to strive so hard to swim, in spite of their blind helplessness.

The remainder of the nest I was allowed to keep, but one by one they began to grow weak and die, much to my parents relief, and my sorrow, which was not a little mixed with guilt at the manner by which I had acquired them. I made graves for them in my garden, amongst the lilies that never flowered, near where we had buried the cockchafer grub.

When a family of civet cats took up residence in the roof space of the bungalow, we heard them lumbering about overhead at night, and Father complained angrily about the noise and the smell for which they were notorious. He decided they must go and to this end, one or two of the local planters were invited over to hunt them. They brought their dogs with them, to drive them out of the roof.

The adult civets and one kitten were killed. Later that day Mother found two more kittens hiding among a clump of ferns that grew against the house. About the size of feline kittens, they were so pretty that she rescued them for us to keep as pets.

It was with great reluctance that Father agreed to this, stipulating firmly. "All right, but only for the time being, as they are still too young to stink like full-grown toddy-cats!"

We called them Castor and Pollux, after the Gemini twins. They were very gentle little creatures, with silky black and brown striped fur and long bushy tails. Their pointed faces and bear-like paws were covered with velvety black fur.

The commode-hutch, placed on its back with the opening at the top, was once more brought into service. Placed this way up, it was unlikely that they could claw their way through the wire door. We fed them with broken dog biscuits and fruit. When we took them out for their daily exercise, unlike the hares, they climbed over us and allowed us to fondle them with no sign of alarm or distress.

Father looked on unenthusiastically whenever he saw us together with them. He had had, it appeared, less qualms over my ratlets! He knew that the time would come, as they matured, when he would have to dispose

Unsuitable Pets

of them. No one ever kept toddy-cats as pets. Their smell was noxious, though used as a base for some of the most expensive perfume, he believed.

We adored the pretty animals, and were convinced that they reciprocated our feelings. However, at this point Fate decreed that we were to have to leave them for a while, which was to change everything.

Father had always been concerned about my health. This may have been because I was beyond the age when most English children were returned to Britain not just because they needed to be educated in English schools, but also because the climate was judged to be unhealthy. I was unfortunate in having a sallow complexion, and a tendency to dark circles below my eyes, which reinforced his conviction that I was, in some undefined way, sickly. My sister and brothers had fair hair and rosy cheeks, while my hair was dark, and my complexion likewise. I do not remember being ill very often, once malaria was eradicated from the District, but it was this concern for my health, which was not extended to Peter, who was regarded as 'wiry', that resulted in the decision that I should have my tonsils removed.

It was, at that time regarded as the normal thing with children. In much the same way that puppies tails were docked, children had their tonsils removed. It was thought to lessen the possibilities of throat infections and colds.

In order to have the operation, it would be necessary for me to go to hospital. This would involve a journey of about one hundred miles to Nargacoil, in the Low Country. Peter and Mother would accompany me.

When the news was broken to me, my main objection was that we would have to leave Castor and Pollux behind. I knew that the dogs and cats would be fed by the servants, and Father would take the dogs for walks; but Kunichin, like Father, regarded the civets as vermin, and disliked them intensely.

"Kunichin will feed and clean them," said Mother, "they will be perfectly all right. We will only be away a week or two."

"But he won't be kind to them." we protested.

"Of course he will. "Mother insisted. "They'll be all right, you'll see. Anyway, we can't take them with us. I'll ask him to take good care of them."

We were not reassured, having in the past, seen Kunichin flicking dishcloths at the cats, but we had to comply, and it was with reluctance we said goodbye when it was time to leave.

JOURNEY TO NARGACOIL

The train for Trivandrum left from Kottayam, a station some distance down the ghat below Vandiperiyar.

We were driven there early one morning by our father, along the narrow zigzagging road through the hills, a steep drop on one side; on the other, high banks and, at intervals, deep pits: the storm drains that prevented the road from flooding during the monsoon. Driving was hazardous, the car unreliable. We edged past bullock carts and lorries going to the bazaar, and drove from tea plantations, through grassland, into jungle, where Peter and I, looking into the tangle of trees and green shadows, were aware of an atmosphere of lurking danger, and hoped the car would not break down! Hidden there, we knew, were plants whose fruit, though it looked temptingly beautiful, could kill if so much as tasted; snakes that either poisoned or strangled; savage animals and stinging insects.

Now and then the jungle was broken by rivers that fell down the mountain in foaming cascades, throwing out rainbows in the sunlight against the dark foliage and granite boulders, dazzling us with their beauty.

Whenever we drove any distance, our mother would make sure we had with us a small white enamel chamber pot, for both Peter and I were prone to car-sickness. The pot, (or chattee,) avoided the necessity of frequent stops. For me, much of the journey passed, as was usual, in a haze of nausea, exacerbated by the constant corkscrewing of the road.

The station itself was at the edge of the jungle, clinging to the hillside. Monkeys swarmed in the trees, awaiting the arrival of the train. As it drew in to the platform, they began their raid; begging and snatching titbits from the passengers; stealing anything they could grab from the carriages and springing back into the trees, where they chattered and quarrelled together over their booty and pelted the train with the remains, like long-tailed demons.

Peter and I found them as wonderfully funny as a circus of clowns. Mother, however, once we were safely installed in our carriage, made sure we kept the door and windows closed, until the train was well under way.

Rail travel was, from my car-sick point of view, a much superior mode of travel. As soon as we had waved Father out of sight, we set about examining our surroundings.

The compartment was panelled in polished wood with fittings of brass. There was a long seat on one wall, which became a bed at night. Above this was a second bunk that folded away into the wall during the day. On the opposite wall we found a small cabinet, which opened downwards to reveal a little brass basin and, folded back inside, a narrow tube, also of brass. When we pulled this down, it produced a thin trickle of water into the basin.

A carafe of drinking water and a glass were also contained within the recess.

In the same wall, a narrow door concealed the lavatory. We pulled a lever in the woodwork, releasing a small cascade of water, while a trapdoor at the bottom of the pan opened on to the track.

All this was new and fascinating to us. We took off our sandals and ran from one window to the other to see the changing landscape, hanging out of the windows to feel the wind in our faces, and watch the other coaches snaking behind and before us as the train curved along the hillsides. We waved to anyone else whose head emerged, until smuts from the engine blew into our eyes.

We were far too excited for even this to discourage us for long. Castor and Pollux, our Heavenly Twin civet cats, were forgotten, left as they were to their fate at Kunichin's hands.

At the start of the journey, the view was of trees, and banana plantations, and here and there small villages with goats and chickens, and naked children who stared at us and sometimes waved. As we descended, the air grew warmer and Mother pointed out coconut and date palms.

There were several short stops at small stations, where passengers alighted and others took their places. Towards evening the train drew in to a larger station. Here we made our way along the platform to the dining-car for our evening meal. The tables were set out with white cloths, polished cutlery and elaborately folded napkins. The waiters were dressed in starched white jackets, their turbans impeccably wound. As we ordered our meal, the train moved on towards the next station.

The passengers, all of whom were Europeans, relaxed formality to introduce themselves and conversation flowed across the tables as Peter and I ate what we could of what was a more elaborate meal than our usual supper.

At the next stop we returned to our carriage to find that in our absence, the bunks had been made up, the oil lamps lit, and a jug of hot water placed by the basin, by invisible hands.

It was almost dark by now. Peter and I washed in the little basin and donned our pyjamas before climbing on to the lower bunk. We lay head to toe and tried not to kick each other, while Mother, on the top bunk, read for a while by the dim glow of the oil lamp.

It took me a long time to go to sleep on the narrow, unfamiliar bed, with Peter's legs beside me. There was the strangeness and excitement of the rhythm of the wheels, the panting engine and the jolting of the carriage as we rolled on into the night. I had never been to a hospital, and though I had been told in general terms what was in store for me, I could not visualise it.

My elder brother, Robert, had had his tonsils removed while we were on leave , 'at home', as our parents referred to it. The doctor had come to the house where we were staying, and carried out the operation on a table that had been placed on the top landing.

The rest of us children were taken out for the day. When we returned the house smelt strongly of disinfectant, and another sickly smell, which I was later to recognise as ether. Robert, lying in bed, looked pale, and was irritable with me, and disinclined to answer my questions. There was a smear of blood on his pillow.

Journey to Nargacoil

The operation, it later turned out, had not been done thoroughly enough. His tonsils grew back, and he had had to go to hospital to have them removed properly, as we learnt from letters from England after our return. This was why I was being taken to Nargacoil, instead of being treated at home by Dr Patterson.

As I thought of all this, and tried not to fidget or kick Peter, I also thought of Castor and Pollux, and hoped they were all right in Kunichin's care. Outside, beyond the stuffy warmth of the compartment, night was pressing against the windows. Looking through the space at the bottom of the blind, I saw showers of sparks, like crimson fireflies, blow past in the smoke. At length I drifted into sleep.

We awoke to the first rays of dawn. We had left the hills and were crossing the plain. On either side of the train, bare red earth stretched to the horizon. Mist was rising from the ground in wispy strands; the sun, not yet visible, had stained the morning sky a delicate pink.

Before long the train reached another stop, where we were to have breakfast while the engine was refuelled. Mother had dressed, but since the air was pleasantly warm, Peter and I, still in our pyjamas, ran barefoot along the cool paving of the platform to the dining car. There was a hubbub of sounds: voices of people leaving the train as they called the porters, doors thumping against the carriages as they were flung open, cases being dropped, footsteps. Every sound was sharper in the early morning air. The second and third class coaches bulged with sari-clad women clutching small children, and turbaned men with thick moustaches. Food-sellers, and porters carrying piled-up suitcases on their heads, hurried along the platform.

Over our breakfast Peter and I watched the crowds, while Mother chatted to the fellow passengers she had met at dinner the previous evening.

By the time breakfast was over, the sun had risen, and the sky had changed to a sheet of metallic blue from horizon to horizon. When it was time to return to our carriage for the last stretch of our journey, Peter and I ran ahead and jumped down on to the platform. Peter went first. Even as my feet touched the paving, I saw him begin to caper madly about, and instantly followed suit, trying vainly to keep both feet off the ground at the same time, shrieking with pain.

Mother was close behind us, and to her astonishment, we both leapt at her and clung to her, our legs wound round her, so that she almost fell.

"It's hot! It's hot!" we screamed, but it was a minute or two before she understood our words.

"Whatever are you doing?" She said, half-laughing, as she tried to prise us off, "Get down, I can't hold you both at once."

The ground, in the short time since the sun had risen, had become a hot-plate, and our bare feet, though toughened from walking about the house and garden without shoes, were unable to stand such heat. Mr Wilshaw's fire-walkers came to mind, but they had only had a short stretch of coals to run across, while our coach was some way down the train.

We were still trying to cling to our mother, still screaming when a young man who had alighted after

Journey to Nargacoil

Mother, saw and understood at once what our predicament was and came to the rescue.

"Where are your shoes?" he asked.

"On the bunk." We told him through our tears and our frenzied caperings.

To our relief, calm and practical, he lifted us up instantly, one under each arm, and transported us safely back to our carriage, with Mother leading the way. Amid our profuse thanks, he hurried back to reach his own compartment before the train moved off, leaving us to nurse our scorched feet.

The rest of the journey was eventful only in the extreme warmth of the day, slightly mitigated by the breeze created by the speed of the train. The dusty red plains flowed monotonously past, their flatness broken here and there by twisted thorn trees, patches of cacti, and termite-mounds that resembled the towers of fantastic castles.

Our journey ended at Trivandrum, where we were met by friends of our parents, with whom we were to spend the night.

Their house was cool and shady. A punka flapped to and fro from the dining room ceiling, kept in motion by a boy who sat in the passage and constantly pulled on the rope that swung the fan above us while we ate lunch. Now and then the punka would slow and gradually cease to move, as the boy grew tired or fell asleep. Our host would shout: "Thomas!" and the fan would begin to move again. We felt sorry for the youth, forced to perform this monotonous task, and were glad when we could go to our room to rest, so that he could be allowed to leave his post.

It was still the cool season, the garden was ablaze with roses, cannas and flowering shrubs, but we, used as we were to the climate of a higher altitude, were uncomfortable in the greater heat of the Low Country.

The next day we were driven to the hospital. We were taken to the main building within the compound to meet the Chief Surgeon, Dr Noble, and his wife, who was also a doctor. Dr Noble was a small, dark man, dapper in a short-sleeved white linen suit was that buttoned to the neck with shiny brass buttons. His energetic briskness was tempered by the warmth of his smile.

His wife, a quiet but confident woman led us to the residential wing to see our room and to meet the nurse who would look after me.

The building was a two-storied house with a wide veranda along the front of both floors. Peter and I, used as we were to life in a bungalow, were pleased that our room was upstairs. Wire screens covered the open side of the balcony to keep out flies and mosquitoes, but the mesh was broken in many places, so did not fulfil its purpose.

Peter and I soon began to explore, and talk to the other people who were waiting for operations. Everyone seemed to welcome us. Like us, many of the patients had relatives accompanying them. On the ground floor there was an Anglo-Indian boy of about seventeen with his mother. He, like me was to have his tonsils removed, but was clearly reluctant, and very nervous.

"I won't let them do it!" He said, "No fear! You can't make me!"

"Hush, Patrick," his mother murmured, "Of course you must have them out. The doctor said so."

Journey to Nargacoil

"No!" he shouted, "I tell you, I won't!"

I was surprised that a grown-up, as he seemed to me, should show his fear like that. I had assumed that being grown-up meant that you were not afraid of anything. Peter and I were expected to at least try to be brave, so surely someone as old as Patrick should not show such panic? I tried to reassure him by explaining to him what, according to my mother, was to happen.

"They give you chloroform to breathe, and you go fast asleep, then you wake up again and it's all over." I told him. "You won't feel anything at all."

He and his mother exchanged amused glances at my reassurances, but he clearly thought, though he was too polite to say so, that I was only a child, and was not even speaking from experience.

I, on the other hand, felt safe in the atmosphere of kindness and efficiency, and, reassured, stopped worrying. After all, I reasoned, this was a proper hospital where things would be done correctly, unlike poor Robert's experience. So when I was taken down to the theatre, I lay trustingly on the table in the white room, and allowed Mrs Noble to put the gauze mask over my face. As requested I slowly began to count to twenty, aware of the sickly smell of ether that filled the air.

I returned to consciousness in my bed in the ward. The smell of ether still filled my mouth. It and my throat hurt. Mother and Nurse Wolf were beside me.

"You're awake then, are you, darling? How do you feel?" Mother asked.

The way I felt was sick! I vomited blood and bile into to basin they held for me. It was not a pleasant awakening, but everyone was solicitous. I was allowed to choose whatever I liked to drink, though just then swallowing was unpleasant and everything seemed to taste of the anaesthetic. I knew now why Robert had been so reluctant to talk to me.

I asked about the boy, Patrick, who had been so scared.

"Has he had his tonsils out too?" I croaked, "Is he all right?"

"Well," said Nurse Wolf, "I'm afraid he wasn't as calm about it you were. It took three people to hold him down, and he threw the mask across the room twice!"

"Why did he do that? Why was he so frightened?" I asked, still amazed that an adult was capable of showing such unrestraint.

"It was rather unfortunate, really. He was next on the list after you, and you were carried out on the stretcher past him, still unconscious. It frightened him. I expect he thought we'd killed you!"

I went down to see him when my throat was less sore. I was feeling smug at being braver than he was. He did not seem very glad to see me. I do not think it helped that his mother held me up as an example of how he should have behaved. However, I had friends among other patients, whom Peter and I visited and chatted to, and had also become very attached to Nurse Wolf, who was making me a dress in her spare time.

We liked to watch the sun-birds, the first we'd ever seen, feeding from a flowering creeper that twined itself over the veranda pillars. There was also Mr Walsh, another of the patients, who had tamed some of the little stripped squirrels that played in the trees outside, and carried them about in his pockets.

Journey to Nargacoil

We stayed at Nargacoil for about ten days, until my throat was judged to be sufficiently healed, but before we returned to Arnakal, Mother took us to spend a day at Kovalum, a place well known as a beauty spot. It was our first visit to the Indian seaside. The sand was white, and coarse, like grains of polished rice. Coconut palms grew at the edge of the sea. We collected cowry shells and found tiny crabs in the rock pools. Although I was forbidden to paddle, Peter and I ran barefoot along the wet sand in the cool sea breeze, and threw pebbles into the waves.

Our journey home was broken by another stay with our parents' friends in Travancore. This time, we were there for several days, and were taken to visit the zoo, which was not far from the house. We went several times, since, of course we fell in love with many of the animals The giraffes were among our favourites, with their lustrous, thickly-lashed eyes and their triangular faces. They stretched their long necks over the railings to eat leaves and grass from our hands.

There were also the gibbons, swinging gracefully across their cages, on extraordinarily long arms; and a pair of lion cubs. We watched the cubs being fed, and later, at the house, we heard them roaring, and mimicked them, as we did with the jackals at Arnakal, to the consternation of our hosts.

In spite of these diversions, we were looking forward to going home, to see how the civets had fared while we had been away.

As soon as we got back, we rushed to their hutch, longing to take them out to cuddle and fuss over. They were alive and well, looking as silky soft as we remembered them, but noticeably larger. We reached out to lift them up, but they cowered back defensively, teeth bared, claws extended, and spat at us. Dismayed and disappointed at our reception after so short an absence, we at once assumed that, as we had feared, Kunichin had tormented them. We tried hard to get them used to us again, talking to them and feeding them ourselves, but to no avail. They no longer trusted humans. Added to which, they had grown so much bigger in the time we were away. Although not yet of fully adult size, they were now as large as domestic cats, and the commode was too small to hold them comfortably, yet they were too fierce to take out for exercise. It was, Peter and I reluctantly had to admit, time for them to go.

Mother knew that we would be heartbroken if they were destroyed. She herself had a sneaking affection for them, for they were attractive animals, and it was she who had been responsible for saving them in the first place.

"If you let them free anywhere round here, they'll move back into the roof again for certain." Father said, "Then we'll have to shoot them, or they'll stink the place out."

We tried hard to think of a solution to the dilemma, and it was Mother who found it.

"We could take them to the jungle," she said, "and let them go there. As long as we go far enough away for them not to find their way back."

This idea pleased us, for they had after all been our friends and had become vicious only through fear, (although Kunichin strongly denied that he had teased them at all.) We had to admit that it was just possible that their wildness could have been due to the fact that they were not exercised or handled while we were away.

However, Peter and I always suspected that our doubts were well founded.

So it was that one day soon after our return, Mother donned her leather gardening gloves for protection, and picked the civets, struggling and protesting, out of the commode, and put them into a smaller packing case, fastening the lid tightly shut. Then, with the box roped to the luggage rack, we drove towards the jungle the other side of Vandiperiyar, far away from any houses. Fortunately the civets were still too young for their scent glands to be active, so they were not yet unpleasant to handle, apart from the danger of being bitten.

As soon as we saw a clearing close to the road, Mother parked the car on the verge. We all got out and lifted the box off the back of the car. As we carried it to the edge of the jungle, we could feel Castor and Pollux struggling to escape.

We put the box on the ground and opened it. Our last sight of the Heavenly Twins was of two patches of black and brown fur, leaping away from us before they disappeared forever into the mass of greenery.

Castor and Pollux were the last of our wild pets, though there were insects such as caterpillars, and the cockchafer larva, which we kept for a while to study.

Once a beautiful pale green praying mantis took up residence on a fern growing up one of the pillars of our veranda. We watched it for days, and fed it titbits from our meals, which it sampled with a genteel grace. Unfortunately one day it moved its position from the fern to a door post. A sudden draught blew the door shut, and thus ended that episode and the mantis's existence.

We grew accustomed, through these small tragedies, to the transience of life amongst these creatures we loved. That at least, they taught us. Of course we still had the dogs and cats, and assorted poultry, but we had also, by that time learnt that wild creatures do not adapt well to being domesticated, and we had no desire, and were not encouraged to keep them like zoo animals, shut in cages to be stared at, and never touched.

Of the dogs, there was Digger, who was the sole survivor of the collection of dogs we had had before the last leave. Part retriever, part Irish terrier, he was a good natured towards people, even if he had killed my rabbit, and tolerated being played with by Peter and me.

Then one day Francis brought us a small black puppy with floppy ears, which he said was sired by one of our neighbour's spaniel. The mother was a pye-dog from the village. We called him Mickey, after Mickey Mouse, who, at that time was only known as a black and white cartoon.

Our adoration of the puppy must have been a bit too enthusiastic, for Mickey soon learnt that he could find peace and quiet only by snapping at us. Before he was full grown, he had decided that he was not going to allow us to stroke or pat him, and was likely to bite us if we tried to insist on caressing him.

Apart from his dislike of being touched, he seemed fond enough of us, always welcomed us with a wagging tail if we had been away without him, and was enthusiastic about coming for walks. In many ways he was another pet that proved unsuitable for domesticating, but he remained faithful in his own way.

THE NIGHT OF THE VAMPIRE

I awoke suddenly and lay still. Protected though I was by the white gauze of the mosquito net, I was afraid. From above me came the sound of wings. Not, I was certain, an insect sound. Neither the maddening high-pitched whine of a mosquito, nor the buzz and thump of bluebottles. These were easy to recognise. Nor was it the soft flutter of moths, who sometimes struggled round the walls and ceiling, vainly trying to escape from the room, but apparently unable to accept the solidity of the whitewashed walls.

I was still dream-befuddled, but I felt the presence of some dark thing hovering above the mosquito net, searching I was sure for a tear or hole through which it could descend upon my helpless body.

The cause of my waking had been my need to relieve myself, but I dared not emerge from the safety of my net-enclosed bed. Under normal circumstances, I would keep my sleepy eyes closed and roll against the net until my body's weight dragged the edge free from under the mattress. I would slide through the gap, until my feet touched the floor, then grope my way to the bathroom. But not tonight. . .I listened to the sound of the unseen wings and could imagine the evil thing waiting for me.

Across the room, in the big wooden cot, also veiled with netting, Peter slept undisturbed. I could hear his breathing that was nearly a snore, but not quite; more a rhythmic sibilance. Steady, regular. It should have reassured me, but instead my terror was for both of us.

At the window the long dark blue curtains bellied and flapped in the night breeze. Crickets were busily making their watch-winding music. Far away, as usual at night, a dog was barking. All familiar noises of the night, but I cringed under the sheet, clutching my pillow for comfort, with my ears straining to hear the dreadful sound. In my imagination a creature hovered there, hideous, sinister. A vampire.

My knowledge of vampires was limited, but the word itself was evocative of something unspeakable.

Mother had taken to reading us snippets from the Madras Mail when we sat with her in the afternoons. There were the reports on Gandhi's latest fast and news from England, but what we liked best were the more colourful items; such as the story of the baby born with two heads, one a child's, the other an owl's, which hooted like that bird; stories of children reared like Mowgli in the Jungle Books, by wild animals; tales of dead people returning to life just as the funeral pyre was being lit; of Siamese twins; of strange plagues; and of vampire bats which attacked people as they slept, and left them sick, debilitated, drained of their blood.

It was, I suppose, unwise of her to expose two imaginative children, such as we were, to these lurid stories. But to her, commonsensical as she was, they seemed so preposterous that she thought they were simply funny, and did not dream that we believed them. And nor did we. Except that we could not help wondering if there might not be just that grain of truth included.

Of bats, we saw plenty, sweeping in circles round the garden at dusk. Once we had found a fruit bat, hanging like a bunch of dusty cobwebs in a dark corner of the spare bathroom. Mother caught it in the butterfly net. We had examined its little foxy face and long delicate suede wings, and looked in the Children's Encyclopaedia to identify it, before we let it go. We had no fear of bats as such. Not ordinary bats at any rate.

But tonight was different. Why didn't it go away? Surely it must soon grow tired and give up, returning the way it had come. But no, in the deep darkness of the curtained room, the sound of those unseen wings paused for a moment, and beat on and on.

My fear increased, as my need to get to the bathroom grew more urgent. I began to cry, and having begun with an unhappy snivel, panic took me over, and I thought how alone and helpless I was, with this terrible, unknown thing fluttering over me, waiting for me to emerge from the fragile citadel of my netted bed. My sobs grew to shrieks.

" Mummy! Mummy! Help, help!"

I heard her at last, stumbling along the veranda that lay between her room and ours, tripping over the toys that we had failed to put away before bedtime. The light of her candle wavered and fluttered before her as she opened the door, her bare feet padding on the stone floor.

"What is it? Darling, what's the matter? Are you ill? Did you have a nightmare?" she pulled up the net and took me in her arms.

"There's a vampire," I sobbed." I heard it. Up there. Right over me!"

It did not occur to me that it might attack her.

Peter, woken by the hullabaloo, was sitting up, rubbing his eyes in the dim light of the candle. Mother held it up to illuminate the walls and ceiling. The shadows flickered back as she slowly circled the room, but there was nothing to be seen except a pair of daddy-longlegs joined together in a corner above my bed.

"It was there." I said vehemently. "I heard it. It went on and on, with huge big wings."

"No, no," she said, kissing me and drying my tears. "You must have been dreaming. I shall have to stop reading you newspaper stories if they make you so frightened."

I choked back my sobs and ceased complaining, for I knew I wanted to hear more of these lurid tales. They were far better than Grimms' Fairy Tales, because of the possibility that they might be true.

After I had been lighted to the bathroom by her candle, and Peter had been reassured that all was well, she tucked me up again, and made certain the mosquito net was securely sealed. I snuggled down under the sheet and watched the light wavering away, until I heard the veranda door snap shut.

Peter asked sleepily, "What happened, Eve?"

"There was a vampire in here," I said, "but it seems to have gone now. You don't have to worry."

And indeed the wings were at silent, and did not return.

DISH OF THE DAY

It was Kunichin who made the oven for us. Peter and I must have expressed a desire to cook something more realistic than meals made from tea-seeds, flowers and stones on pretend fires, so Kunichin created a tiny outdoor stove for us out of two dog biscuit tins. In that humid climate many things came in tins; our father's Gold Flake cigarettes; sweets; biscuits. Dog-biscuits came in deep, square tins with a circular lid in the top and " Spratt's Dog Biscuits " in large letters on the sides.

Kunichin dug a shelf in a bank of earth at the back of the kitchen garden, behind the New Stable, which held no horses, only the lawn mowers and garden rollers. He placed the tins side by side on this ledge, open side outwards, and cut a hole in the top surface of one with a tin-opener. Over this hole he placed a short piece of iron pipe that was lying about nearby, to act as a chimney. The other tin was to be the oven and hot plate.

He modelled his creation on the wood range in the kitchen with its open fire next to the oven. Having secured the chimney in position with mud and stones, he laid the fire with a handful of dry twigs and leaves.

Dish of the Day

During all this time, as was his way, he said little, but he seemed pleased with the result and our gratitude. It must have been a day when he was feeling better disposed towards us, or perhaps he thought that it would keep us out of mischief for a while.

As a final gesture, he took the spade he had used for making the ledge, and with it collected red-hot charcoal from the kitchen range and tipped it into the biscuit tin oven. The twigs and grass blazed and smoke began to curl out of the chimney, and from the mud 'gasket' round its base.

For a time we were happy, hunting for more fuel for the fire, gathering twigs and grass from round about. However we wanted to cook real food, so we collected one or two cigarette tins which were cylindrical and a convenient size to serve as saucepans; the lids of the dog-biscuit tins we thought we could use as frying pans. But what were we to cook?

The first thing that came into our minds was rice. Neither of us liked rice-pudding, but we both enjoyed eating boiled rice, so we went to the kitchen and begged Francis to let us have a handful of rice grains. He kindly added a spoonful of sugar and some water, and we returned happily to our stove, only to find that in our absence the fire had died.

We tried to revive it by blowing on the ashes, but to no avail.

"Let's get some more charcoal from the kitchen," Peter said.

So we took the spade and went to ask Kunichin to bring us another shovelful of embers, but Muttu shook his head and Francis said, "No." The range was newly stoked in order to heat the oven, so that Muttu could cook our lunch, and he had no interest in fuelling our little fire.

How could we cook without fire? Disconsolately, we went to find Mother to beg a box of matches. These were stored in a cupboard in our parents' bedroom.

"You can have just one box," she said, "you'd better make them last." And then she added, " I hope you won't help yourselves to more when I'm not here, will you? " seeming to be unaware of the fact that such an idea would never have occurred to us had she not mentioned it.

She came with us to admire Kunichin's handiwork, and showed us how to twist pieces of newspaper to kindle the fire, then she found a rag for us to use to lift the saucepan tins off when they were hot.

It took several matches to light the stove as they kept blowing out in the breeze; however we succeeded in the end, and found enough twigs to keep it going until the water began to bubble. We took turns at stirring the rice with a stick, but it rapidly boiled dry and began to scorch. We managed to pull it off the stove, and when it had cooled a bit, we sampled our first attempt at cooking.

Besides being burnt, the rice had not had time to cook, and was still hard. We tried to convince ourselves that it was delicious, but the acrid, smoky taste and the hardness of the grains made it inedible, so we threw it away, scattering it among the plantain trees that grew nearby.

For the next few weeks we experimented with cooking. The matches did not last long. It always took several to light the fire each time, which constantly went out while we searched for more fuel, so though Francis

Dish of the Day

and Kunichin gave us the ingredients we requested for cooking, we needed to solve problem of fire-lighting.

There was the woodshed situated between the stable and the kitchen veranda where a fire usually smouldered within a circle of large stones. On it stood a kerosene can full of water warming in preparation for washing of dishes and so forth. This had been where I had gone to practice smoking, using my own invention of cigarette substitute, which I made by stuffing a short length of bamboo with feathers and dead leaves. The bamboo cigarette would continually go out, and the smoke from the woodshed fire made my eyes stream, so I was soon discouraged from this attempt to imitate my father's habit.

The logs that kept the woodshed fire burning were too large by far to use in our stove, so we found long twigs and held the ends in the fire until they began to flame, then rushed to poke them into the stove to light the leaves and torn newspaper we had put there in preparation. More times than not the twig had gone out before we got there, but usually, with persistence we succeeded in the end.

Peter and I had been warned frequently of the dangers of fire, and told that we must never carry burning sticks about in case a spark set our clothes alight. That we were now allowed to play with our dog biscuit tin oven was a token of Mother's trust in our obedience and our good sense not to do anything rash.

However, we had seen no other way to achieve our aim to cook our own food, though it cost us a great deal of patience.

There was an alternative that occurred to us, but it too was forbidden. I do not know how Mother thought we lit our stove, perhaps she thought we asked Kunichin to do it for us. Perhaps she was happy for us to be so apparently innocently busy that she did not question the ways and means.

On Tuesday afternoons Mother went to play tennis at the Club in Peermade, and was joined there by Father in the evening for bridge. On the other days she always took us for a walk in the cooler part of the afternoon, unless we preferred to play down by the hollow tree, or in the garden.

After Kunichin made us the stove, we usually spent Tuesday afternoons cooking, and we began to get more proficient at producing food that was just about edible and not scorched. Peter was good at making toast, and I began to experiment with fried onions.

As with our preference for plain boiled rice as opposed to the milk pudding, so we liked onions fried but hated them boiled. I used the lid of the dog biscuit tins as a pan in which to fry them. Everything tasted of smoke, which added to the attraction.

However, the length of time it took us to get the stove alight was a major drawback, and so it was that one Tuesday the thought of the matches that Mother had said we were not to help ourselves to, came into our minds. The temptation was irresistible.

There was a stiff breeze that afternoon, and the burning sticks blew out every time we tried to carry them from the woodshed to the stove. Unable to resist any longer, and safe in the knowledge that there was no one about to see us, we climbed through the bedroom window and went to the cupboard. It was often locked but on that day by a happy chance the key was in the lock.

Dish of the Day

We unlocked the door and took a matchbox from the packet. Mother did not miss the box, but until we had used them up, our guilt added a piquancy to our still slightly singed dishes

After the matches had been used up, we did not feel like adding to our burden of guilt by stealing more, but were anxious to solve the problem of fire-lighting, and did so by discovering a barrel of tar near the woodshed.

We found that if we dipped the end of a stick into the tar, and lit that in the shed, it flared like a torch until we reached the stove. From then on we used these tar torches to light the oven. Our guardian angels must have been kept busy, but we managed to avoid setting ourselves alight in the process.

We mentioned the tar barrel at lunch one day.

"I'd forgotten that was there." Mother said.

"I hope you won't try playing with that stuff," said Father, "It's filthy stuff. You'll get it all over your clothes and ruin them if you so much as touch it. And it's inflammable, so don't get it anywhere near the fire, it burns like blazes. Keep away from it, do you hear?"

"Yes," Mother said, "Leave the tar alone."

But, when we were sure no one was looking, we continued to dip our sticks into the barrel and ignite them in the fire in order to kindle our stove.

We felt some pride in our achievements in the area of cooking, and longed for Mother to sample our products, but she always put us off with excuses.

"Thank you so much, darling," she would say, "It looks delicious. Perhaps I'll have it later."

We were sure that, if only we could persuade her to taste it, she would be truly impressed and agree that it really was ambrosia. Fried onions on toast, I thought, was a meal fit for the gods.

One Tuesday I managed to produce a particularly succulent dog biscuit tin lidful of unburnt fried onions, and Peter had toasted a piece of bread to a beautiful golden brown. Uniting the two, we laid the result on a piece of plantain leaf.

It looked so tempting, it was hard not to eat it then and there, but we had decided that this would be for our mother. Surely she would not be able to resist tasting something that looked and smelled so divine?

We took it to Francis.

"Please Francis," I said, "We made this for Mummy. Will you keep it warm for her to have when she gets home? We made it as a surprise for her."

Francis cast a doubtful eye over the square of toast with its coating of onion rings.

"All right," he said, unenthusiastically.

"Please promise, Francis," we urged, "and you're not to forget. You've got to give it to her as soon as she gets home. Please."

"Yes, yes, Missy." Said Francis, and carried the toast and onions to the kitchen.

We were in bed and asleep by the time our parents returned. Our last thoughts had been of the look of surprise and pleasure on Mother's face when she received our gift. We pictured how our skill at cooking would amaze her.

In the morning, when she woke us, we waited for her to mention this, and anticipated her thanks, but she said nothing.

"Did Francis give you a present from us?" we asked.

"No. What was that darling?"

"It's a surprise, but you'll love it," we said.

She called Francis and asked him to bring whatever it was we'd left for her. Francis gave us a long look before he departed reluctantly and returned with a small plate on which our offering was lying. It was, by now, naturally, stone cold, the toast seemed to have shrunk, and looked hard and greasy, the onions had withered into little wrinkled curls.

"You were supposed to keep it warm !" I said accusingly to Francis. "We made it especially for you," we told Mother, "Please, will you just taste it?"

She looked at the faded remains of our former triumph and laughed.

"Oh, how delicious !" She said as she took it from the plate, and our hopes rose. Then she looked at the dog, which was standing beside her, and added: "I think Digger will enjoy it."

She dropped it into his eager jaws. He swallowed it in a single gulp.

Disgust and disillusion swept over us at our inability to impress her. After that, we grew tired of the unreliability of our little stove, and soon were bored with cooking, becoming involved in new games. But we did not forget the sight of our mother tossing our gift to the dog as if it meant nothing.

She had been unable to see that it had been the best thing we had cooked, and we had wanted her to have it for that reason. We did not have the ability to articulate that, and she never understood how deeply our feelings had been wounded.

Father, Peter and Eve at Arnakal

Mother by the stream

The Tea Factory

Father on the estate

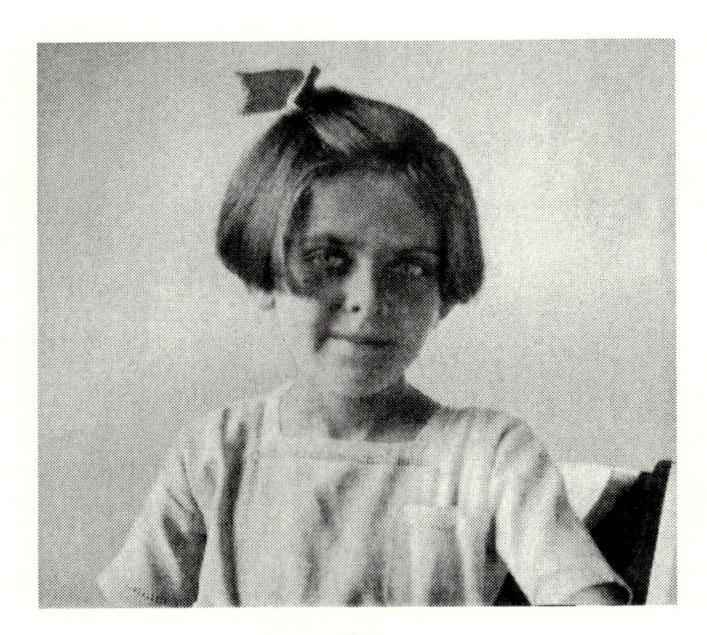

Eve

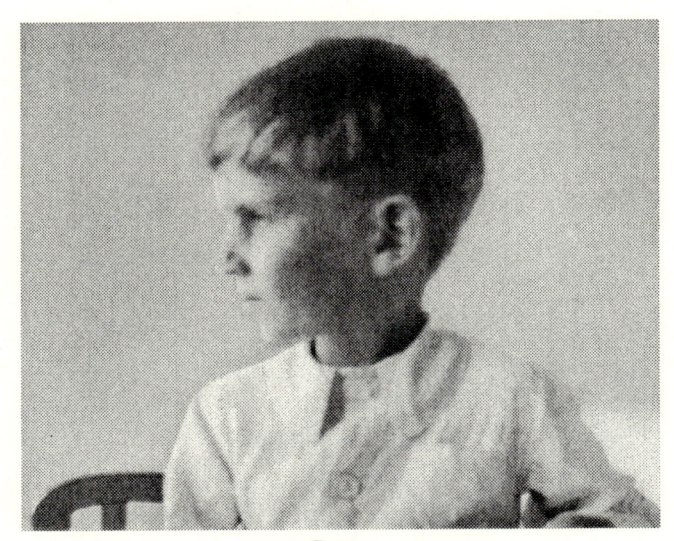

Peter

Father in the sitting room

*The Tennis Party
(father and mother on the left)*

Totemcuran with Peter and Eve in the boat

Elephants at work

The tiger

JACKO

In the evenings, while we were being bathed, especially on moonlit nights, we would hear jackals howling. It was a familiar but eerie sound. First the leader would start up a series of high-pitched yelps ending in a long-drawn howl. The pack would follow with a chorus of yelps, the sound reverberating over the hills.

Peter and I would mimic them, yelping and howling together. We had been told that the jackals were singing: "I smell the body of a dead Hindoo-oo." and the pack were yelping: "Where? Where? Where?"

We would pause from our own howling and listen for them to reply, for we were certain that reply they did, and convinced that each time they sounded closer to us. We would giggle nervously, excited by our power to call them to us, but at the same time, terrified lest they reached the garden and surrounded the house.

We knew them as sinister inhabitants of the night, hunting singly and in packs, feasting on carrion, but also, we believed, capable of stealing children.

There had been an incident, long ago, that I had never forgotten. It took place one day before we had gone on

Jacko

leave to England. The Old Bungalow was being pulled down to make way for the present house, and we were living in the Little Bungalow across the valley, where Mr Wilshaw now resided. I was not yet five years old, Peter almost three, and we were playing on the gravel drive to the side of the house. Peter was collecting pebbles and examining each one, and I had a new doll, a Christmas present, that I was playing with. We were alone, everyone else seemed to have been busy elsewhere.

Then something attracted my attention. I looked up to see a jackal on the top of the bank above the garden, looking down towards us, its ears pricked; a sandy, foxy-looking animal, with pointed ears and muzzle, its bright eyes fixed on Peter, as he sat on the path absorbed in his finds.

While I was watching it, it suddenly jumped down and began to move towards him.

I began to scream, "Its a jackal! Ayah! Ayah! Quick!"

Kunichin and Francis came running out from the kitchen, waving their arms and shouting. The animal turned and fled the way it had come, bounding back over the bank, and disappearing into the plantation.

Peter, startled by the commotion, burst into tears and was scooped up by Francis and carried into the safety of the house. He probably understood very little of the incident, but it made a lasting impression on me. I had known instinctively that jackals were dangerous wild animals. Besides which, I did not like their predilection for decaying creatures and human corpses. It was, however, rare to see them during the day.

The Tea Planter's Children

Sometime after our return from England, Mr Gowan, the Chief Assistant, or S.D., went on leave. His place was filled temporally by Mr Knight, who moved into his bungalow.

Our mother took us with her when she called on him to welcome him to the District and to invite him to dinner in order to introduce him to the other European residents.

We soon realised that Mr Knight was a pleasant but eccentric young man. He had brought with him a collection of unusual pets. Besides an amiable black labrador called Sambo, he owned a green parrot, a young monkey, and a jackal cub. The parrot, Mr Knight claimed could speak, but it declined to do so in our company. It sat on its perch and eyed us, head on one side, distrustfully. Its beak looked capable of delivering a nasty peck, so we did not go near it.

He released the jackal, a half-grown cub, from its kennel, and it squirmed towards us, ears and tail down, fawning. We picked it up, but it bit us with its needle-sharp teeth, so we put it down again and contented ourselves with stroking its coarse, dry fur, that was so unlike the softness of puppy fur.

"I call him Jacko." Mr Night said.

The monkey had been sitting in a large, square cage, silently watching us. Mr Night took it out and fastened a chain round its waist. Its expression seemed to me disapproving, like that of a humourless old man. It brought back a memory of my terror when, as a three-year old, I awoke from my afternoon rest to find the cook's pet monkey sitting on my pillow, grooming my hair.

Jacko

Old Ayah had been seated by my bed, calmly mending my clothes, apparently taking no notice, despite my screams. She, herself was afraid of the monkey, so would not touch it, but called Mother who picked it up and carried it away.

Peter, a baby at the time, had loved the monkey, as had my elder brother, but I was terrified of it.

This monkey was the same species, a rhesus, common in India. Mr Knight let go its chain and it leapt away into a nearby tree, rejoicing in its liberty. To our surprise, he removed his shoes and socks, then left us with the jackal for company, to climb into the tree after it. For a while we watched them swing from branch to branch, chasing each other up and down the tree. In amazement, we watched this simian display from an adult European until after a bit he recaptured the monkey and chained it up again.

Peter and I decided that we liked this strange newcomer. However, we did not see him or his menagerie often, or get to know him well. He seemed to keep to himself a lot, preferring the company of his animals.

A few months later, Peter and I were invited to spend a few days at Munjamully. The Cargils had left to run another tea estate in the High Waveys, and they had been replaced by a young couple, John and Mary Ward, who had asked us to stay with them.

Mary had a three-month old baby, and was much preoccupied with that, and with running the house, so we were left a good deal to our own devices. Being used to amusing ourselves, we invented games to play among the trees and shrubs in the garden.

Mr Gowan's bungalow was quite close to Munjamully, and to our joy, soon after our arrival, Jacko made an appearance. Evidently Mr Knight had decided that the jackal was old enough, and tame enough to run free. He began to turn up almost every day, emerging out of the tea plantation that surrounded the garden. Obsequious though he was and in spite of his nervous excitability, and we were glad to see him and flattered that he seemed to like us. That was before the accident.

It so happened that the Wards had lived for a while in Africa. The house was decorated with souvenirs of their time there, amongst which was a whip. It was a heavy whip, the handle about two feet long, covered in greyish black leather The lash, also of the same leather tapered for some eight feet or so. Made of rhinoceros hide, we were told that it was designed to crack over the backs of teams of oxen when driving them across the veldt.

We soon learnt to swing the lash so that it cracked as loudly as a gunshot. It was a most satisfying sound, and we were fascinated by it. We would stand in the centre of the lawn where we usually played, because it was in sight of the nursery, so Mary's ayah could keep an eye on us. There we practised ways of wielding the whip.

Sometimes we pretended we were part of a circus, and took turns for one of us to be the ringmaster with the whip, while the other was the performing horse or lion.

Once, while I was ringmaster, I accidentally caught Peter's leg with the tip of the thong.

With a shriek, he collapsed, clutching his calf. Throwing down the whip, full of remorse, I tried to comfort him. There was a scarlet weal on the back of his leg. Luckily for me, Mary Ward and ayah were busy bathing the baby, so were unaware of what had happened, and we did not tell them, knowing that if we did so the whip would be taken

Jacko

away. I do not know how we accounted for the mark on Peter's leg. Perhaps no one noticed.

That day, after the initial pain subsided, and Peter's tears had dried, we played a different game.

A day or two later, I again had the whip when Jacko appeared out of the bushes, and came frisking towards us. I was in the process of swinging the lash, circling it round above my head, as he trotted on to the lawn, ears down, tongue lolling, expecting to be welcomed.

"Go away, Jacko!" I shouted, but the sound of his name only made him run more quickly towards me. The lash was curving through the air as Jacko ran into its trajectory, and as it wound itself round his hindleg, he gave a long, high scream, and leapt whimpering away. We rushed towards him, to caress him, to see how badly he was hurt, and to reassure him that I had not meant to injure him. I was mortified by what I had done, but he fled from us, running on three legs into the plantation, and vanished towards his home. We thought we ought to confess to Mr Knight so he could look after Jacko and see to his leg, but we had no way of reaching him. In vain we hoped the cub would come back to us.

It was some days before the jackal reappeared, and then he would no longer come near enough to us for us to stroke him. He did not trust us any more, but lurked in the bushes, and when we were not looking, stole our toys and dropped them among the tea bushes. Sometimes we found them again quickly but sometimes it was not until several days later, when they would be dew-soaked and muddy. Peter had a glove puppet in the form of a monkey that ended up that way, and his Sunny Jim vanished forever, which had a certain irony, after the difficulty we

The Tea Planter's Children

had had, stealing the doll back from Betty. We thought Jacko was taking his revenge, but though we felt that it was deserved, it was upsetting just the same.

After that, we stopped playing with the rhinoceros hide whip. It seemed too dangerous.

When it was time to go home again, we told no one what had happened. I had a great sense of shame that I had hurt Jacko, but could do nothing to remedy what I had done, so I did not tell Mother. Peter, too, remained silent on the subject.

We still howled back in answer to the wild jackals when we heard them. Somehow we had never regarded Jacko as one of their sinister fellowship.

THE SLEEPING PRINCE

When we were disobedient the servants would threaten that tigers would come and eat us up, but we regarded this as an empty threat. We had only seen tigers in pictures, or as rugs on our neighbours' floors, which proved their existence. However, our parents assured us that they were only to be found in deep jungle, well away from the bungalow.

Of course there were times, as in the incident at Munjamully when our imaginations took control and we frightened ourselves with the thought of tigers lurking in the darkness.

Then it happened one day that we overheard talk that a bullock had been taken by a tiger in an outlying village. It was some way from the bungalow and unlikely to be a danger to us but the villagers were alarmed.

A few days later it attacked again, killing a cow, so look-out platforms were built and watches organised. Yet still, from time to time the tiger continued to maraud the same herd, always eluding the watchers.

The Tea Planter's Children

When he had first come to Peermade district, Father, in common with the other planters in the district, hunted in the surrounding jungles and killed his share of big game. There was the bearskin on the sitting-room floor on whose thick black fur Peter and I liked to play. There were also two huge python skins, mounted on black felt with scalloped edges, as well as the heads of a bison and an antelope on the walls. However he had never shot a tiger; in fact it was a long time since he had shot animals for sport, and there was a reason for this.

Mother told us of the day he had tracked down a wild buffalo, a magnificent bull. The animal was standing silhouetted against the sky at the top of a cliff. Father took aim and fired, but in his excitement he only succeeded in wounding it with his first shot. Before he could take aim again, the animal turned and leapt out over the rim of the precipice and crashed to its death a hundred feet below.

"He was so shocked," Mother said, "It was such a waste. It had been such a beautiful creature, and so brave. He couldn't think of hunting as sport any more."

However, to the villagers, of course, the cattle were valuable, and fundamental to their way of life. Besides, they were afraid that the tiger would turn from cattle to people. It was clear that unless the tiger moved back into the jungle, it would have to be destroyed.

Peter and I listened to the talk with interest. We had seen observation platforms elsewhere; flimsy wooden structures high up in trees, reached by bamboo ladders, and positioned where there was good visibility, in jungle clearings, or near open land.

The Sleeping Prince

We also knew that a goat would be tethered near the tree to lure the tiger. We felt deep sympathy for the innocent victim, which would certainly be killed.

The men from the village took turns to sit up all night to await the marauder. The talk went on for several days, as the tiger continued to avoid the lure, so a full scale hunt with beaters and a team of local planters was being planned.

Then, early one morning we were woken by the sound of excited voices. A crowd of coolies came up the path by the vegetable garden and into the kitchen compound, an area of beaten earth behind the house with one or two shade trees, where the chickens scratched during the day.

"They've got the tiger!" Peter shouted.

We saw that the men were carrying a litter made of branches and a piece of corrugated iron. On it lay the body of a huge tiger. They laid it down beneath a tree. Together with our parents we hurried round to see it.

It lay on its side, eyes closed as if asleep. The morning sun cast a dappled shade on the painted silk of its hide. From where we stood there was no sign of the fatal wound.

It had been shot just after dawn by the village headman, or kangani, who stood beside his prize, proud and dignified.

I stared at the beautiful, fearful thing, lying so peacefully there under the tree. The soft fur of the belly, the colour of rich cream, was towards us. The back and upper part of the head were reddish shading down to pale yellow, with the black stripes painted with precision to follow the contours of the shoulders and flanks, and on the face, enhancing the size of the golden eyes that were now closed forever. It looked as if it was smiling. It was the most wonderful creature I had ever seen. . . An enchanted prince from a fairy tale.

Father congratulated the Kangani, who explained how he had shot it. It was a young animal, in its prime, nine feet from the tip of its nose to the end of its striped tail.

Neither Peter or I had seen a real tiger before, and it seemed that it was also an object of wonder to the local populace, who were jostling for a glimpse from beyond the barbed wire fence that divided the compound from the tea plantation. They were a bright mass of orange, pink and blue saris and white dhotis against the dark green bushes.

Francis, Kunichin, Muttu and the gardener stood behind us, in silent awe.

The skin was offered to our father and a price negotiated. The Kangani kept the whiskers, probably already removed for they were regarded as possessing powerful magic.

When, at last, the congratulations were over and the price agreed, Mother took some photographs with her Box Brownie camera.

After that the work of skinning must begin at once, before the sun rose higher and the day grew hot. Already the flies were beginning to swarm round the corpse.

We were led away, but saw the first cut along the belly. The pale fur parted in a pink line, exposing the paunch. Our father had explained how the skin should be cut so that it could be removed in one piece. The smell of blood and tiger, musky, cat-like, was increased as the paunch was opened. We hurried away, retching.

Later, curiosity drew us back. By then the magnificence that had dazzled us that morning, was reduced to a pile of blood-stained skin and fur, and a crimson corpse, raw and naked. Nearby was a heap of stinking entrails. The flies had gathered in their thousands.

The carcass was rapidly dismembered, the flesh hung on the spikes of the barbed wire fence and sold to the waiting crowd, which had, like the flies, multiplied considerably as the news had spread.

Peter and I, though the smell and sight still disgusted us, paused on the kitchen veranda in silent amazement. We had no idea that anyone could eat a tiger. Of course, the people were very poor. Meat was a luxury, and above all, they probably believed that the flesh of such a beast had great potency.

It was a gruesome end to the beautiful creature that had lain as if asleep there on the dark earth that morning. The ground where it had lain was crimson, and the flies were feasting on the spilled blood.

The skin was sent to Madras to be cured, and later returned. In spite of being rubbed with salt and ashes before the journey, it was slightly damaged by maggots, and not perfect, though it was still a fine skin. The head was not stuffed or mounted as was often the custom, so that the ears were flattened, the once smiling face, a wrinkled mask. It was an ornament, a decorative floor covering, lying beside the bearskin and the two pythons on the drawing room floor.

But beside the memory of that sleeping beauty, it was little more than an old fur coat, the discarded clothing of the prince it had adorned. Only a skin, after all.

THE JUJU CAT

"Here you are. I expect you would like this." Mother said, handing me a small object. She had been tidying the 'odds-and-ends' drawer in her writing desk.

"I never throw anything away," she would say, "It's sure to come in useful within seven years." So her drawer contained every sort of odd screw or bolt, picture-hooks, paperclips, pen-nibs, stubs of pencil, nails and ends of sealing wax. Somehow this little object had found its way amongst them.

"What is it?" I asked, looking at it. It seemed to be made of black glass.

"I think it's supposed to be a lucky black cat." She said. "It must have come from a cracker. It's a lucky charm, a mascot."

She laughed as she spoke, for she was too down-to-earth and practical to believe that a small glass animal could influence anyone's fortune.

I regarded it suspiciously, for I did not share her realistic outlook, and I thought the little glass creature looked evil. Perhaps that was to some extent due to its colour but it was also the expression on its tiny face. It

The Juju Cat

was only about an inch high, with two staring green eyes painted on the narrow end that represented the head, and a bad-tempered, down-turned mouth. The little ears were chipped as if it had taken part in many battles with other black glass cats. I distrusted it.

"That can't be a lucky charm," said Peter when I showed it to him," It looks like a juju."

He laughed a lot at the word, and also at the idea of an unlucky mascot.

I wanted to throw it away, but I was afraid that if I hurt its feelings, it would find a way to get back at me.

"It's SUPPOSED to be a lucky black cat." I told him, "It can't help being ugly."

I hid it in a box of crayons, for want of anywhere better. At least, in a box, its staring eyes would not be watching me. I thought: "Peter's probably right. It's a juju. It's come to bring us bad luck." I wondered whether, if I could make myself like it, it might become lucky, but I did not trust it. It had such a look of wickedness.

After a time I forgot about it, though it would reappear whenever I opened the box to use my crayons.

It so happened that soon after I was given the Juju-talisman, my cat, Tiddles gave birth to a litter of kittens. We had two cats at that time; Tiddles and her son, a ginger tom belonging to Peter. They were, in the main, aloof creatures who sometimes consented to being cuddled or stroked, but protested at being dressed in dolls clothes, and kept their distance. This was also because they distrusted the dogs, who chased them whenever they saw them.

Tiddles had her kittens in a box up above the store room in the kitchen annex. There was no ceiling here, just rafters resting on the external walls to support the roof.

The interior walls rose to a height of about eight feet and were a foot or so thick, and level along the top.

Peter and I heard the kittens squeaking, and clambered up the store room shelves to find them. Once we realised that Tiddles had given birth, we watched carefully until she left them to get her food, before we climbed up again to inspect them.

There were four kittens, all tabby and white like their mother.

We climbed up and walked along the tops of the walls almost every day to see how they were developing.

The other side of the store room wall were the servants rooms. We avoided looking into them, as a rule, because we felt we were trespassing on their privacy, though they were rarely in the rooms at that time of day. The rooms were starkly simple in their furnishing; just a camp bed and their box of clothes. The walls were whitewashed, the floors mud, sealed with a wash of cow-dung.

After about a week Tiddles and the kittens vanished. Probably she had seen our visits and wanted to hide them from us. Or it could have been that the box they were in was too small. For a few days we did not know where they had gone, then once more the kittens' cries gave them away. This time they were in the wide galvanised iron hopper-head below the gutters of the walkway that joined the kitchen to the bungalow.

We fetched a ladder and climbed up to see them. Dead leaves had accumulated in the hopper, blocking the down-pipe, and forming a comfortable mattress. Since it was the dry season, there was little threat that they would be washed away by a sudden downpour. The kittens had grown, and their eyes were beginning to open.

The Juju Cat

We visited them once or twice during the next few days, and then were preoccupied with other things for a day or two.

On my next visit, I noticed as I put the ladder in place, that they were silent. I wondered if I should find that Tiddles had moved them again. I peeped over the edge of the hopper and saw that Tiddles was not there. The kittens lay motionless, sprawled as if asleep. I picked up the nearest. It was obviously quite dead, as were the other three.

Shocked, I called Peter, who climbed up beside me. Then we ran, dismayed, to tell Mother.

"Perhaps the father came and killed them," she said. "The father must have been a wild cat. If they find their kittens I'm told they usually kill them. They are very jealous. Or, of course it may simply have been too hot for them there at midday. There can't be any shade up there."

"Can we bury them?" I asked. The thought of the funeral consoled us more that a little. "Can we borrow your trowel?"

"It might be better to ask Totemcurran to do it." She advised, "They must be buried deeply enough, or their mother will smell them and dig them up again."

"We'll do it properly. We really will. Of course we will," we protested. "We'll make a really deep hole for them."

"All right, if you're sure, but the ground will be quite hard now. You'd better find a place in one of the flowerbeds where it's been dug already. You'll find it easier there."

However, we decided that the grave should be beneath the bottlebrush mimosa tree. The branches hung down like a roof. We liked to play houses under it because we were quite hidden within it. The ground was always soft, thickly carpeted with the fallen leaves that had accumulated over many years.

Unfortunately, when we began to dig, we found that the mat of leaf mould was felted together in a tough resistant layer. We managed to scrape it away until we reached the underlying soil but this was not only dry and hard, but contained a web of roots and fibre, impeding our efforts to make a sufficiently deep hole to contain the kittens. We dug away as best we could, getting hot and sweaty through our endeavours, until we had penetrated down barely a foot.

"Surely," I said, "that will be deep enough, won't it?"

Peter, who was getting as discouraged as I was, agreed, though a little doubtfully.

We had wrapped the tiny corpses in leaves and now laid them in the hole, scattering a few mimosa flowers over them before we scraped the soil back on top of them. Being dust-dry and full of leaf mould, it would not pack down well. I had an uneasy feeling that we should have dug deeper, but we were by then too hot and tired to do more.

We made up a sort of prayer that we said over the grave, and laid a few more flowers on the top of the little dusty heap before we left.

"Tiddles won't know they're here anyway." I said, to ease my conscience, but as we emerged from beneath the canopy of the bush, she was sitting washing her paws at the edge of the lawn.

"I expect it will be all right," Peter said.

The Juju Cat

But when we went back the next morning to inspect the grave we found the four little bodies strewn about the lawn. By now they were stiff and seemed to have grown larger, swollen in the process of decomposing. Flies were swarming round them.

When we had buried the kittens, their soft fluffiness had disguised, to some extent, their deadness. Now I was filled with dread at the sight of them, partly compounded by my guilt that we had not buried them deeply enough. They had become hideous and we could neither of us find the courage to pick them up and rebury them. In fear and horror we ran away and left them to putrefy where they lay amid the flies.

Later Mother asked the gardener to bury them at the back of a flower bed, as she had at first suggested.

After that I could not go to that part of the garden. I was sure that the ghosts of the kittens were waiting there to accuse me.

When next I opened my box of crayons, the juju-cat fell out and looked at me with its hard green stare, and what seemed to me a self-satisfied smirk. I had forgotten its existence. I put it quickly back in the box, wondering what other evil spells it was concocting. I tried to think of a way to lose it, but nothing came to mind.

EXPEDITIONS

There were many walks around the bungalow, and almost all were beside streams for in that hilly place, nowhere was far from the sound of running water. Often we would scramble down the steeply terraced hill near the house to a wide stream. This was spanned by two long planks which formed a simple bridge. Above the bridge the water flowed down through a grove of eucalyptus trees, whose mottled trunks and grey-green leaves shaded and were reflected in the water. Below, the stream tumbled over an outcrop of rocks, forming shallow pools in which we could safely paddle. Often as we walked, Mother would tell us tales of the 'olden days', one of which was about an accident that had once happened at the bridge.

It had taken place when I was a baby, before Peter was born, a time when we still had horses. Robert had been on his pony, Brownie, led by Nulla Tumby, the horse-coolie. Ann, aged at the time about three and a half, was on Mother's pony, a docile grey called Sally, with Mother leading her. Since Mother rode side-saddle, the pommel was handy for us to hold on to when we were small. Also in the party was Kunichin, twelve years old then, and employed to help Ayah to look after us.

On reaching the stream, Nulla Tumby waded across at a shallow place leading Brownie. Mother, however, did not want to stop to remove her shoes and stockings.

"I decided to lead Sally across the bridge," she told us, "I was sure I had ridden her over it before."

The bridge was about three feet wide by twelve feet long.

"I was walking across the bridge with my hand behind me on the reins, when suddenly Sally must have put one foot over the edge. I looked round to see her falling heavily into the water. She began to plunge about in fright. Luckily Ann was thrown clear, and landed up to her neck in the stream some feet away. Her topee had fallen off and was sailing down to the rocks. With great presence of mind, Kunichin jumped in and rescued her, while Nulla Tumby ran back and caught Sally."

It seemed that they had had an extraordinarily lucky escape. Had the water been shallower, or had Sally fallen to the other side among the rocks, without doubt, it would have ended in tragedy. As it was, apart from the shock, and the drenching, the only damage was a small tear in the leather of the pommel!

Here below the bridge we would spend the morning playing naked in the rock pools, while Mother sat under a tree and read or sewed.

The walk we enjoyed least was up the avenue, past the factory and through the Lines, for here inevitably, we collected a swarm of native children, naked save for a medallion dangling from a string round their rice-inflated bellies. They would follow us, chattering and giggling together at the sight of our pale skins and our, in their eyes, bizarre clothes.

Maddened by this uninvited retinue, we would turn and shout: "Ordi! Ordi por! Go away!"

It was always futile. The children would stop with screams of laughter, and as soon as we turned round, they fell in behind us again. It was a game of Grandmother's footsteps. When we went forward, they followed, when we stopped and turned round, they froze where they were. Sometimes, driven to desperation, we would pick up sticks from beside the road and threaten to hit them, but this merely provoked more merriment as they scattered, just out of reach, only to reform again as soon as our backs were turned. It was an ordeal we dreaded. Through it all Mother walked ahead with the dogs, apparently oblivious of our discomfort. Eventually she would turn to wait for us.

"Hurry up," she would say, "Take no notice of them, they'll soon go away."

In the end, the village grandmothers, left in charge of the children while their mothers were working, would come out of the grass huts where they lived, and call them back.

A route we sometimes took after we had passed the Lines, was through a plantation where the women would be working, moving slowly among the tea bushes in their bright saris. As they went, they picked the tender young shoots, tossing them, in handfuls over their shoulders into the bamboo baskets on their backs. The white-clad overseers, or kanghanis went from group to group checking that they took only the tips of the shoots, and instructing the novices in what they did.

At the bottom of the hill on which that plantation grew, ran a river where the dhobi washed our clothes. As we approached, we could hear the slap-slap-slap of cloth being beaten on the flat rocks that made this the chosen washing place. As soon as we rounded the bend, the slapping ceased suddenly, and there was the little dhobi man, his loin cloth tucked up between his legs, crouched at the water's edge, rubbing the clothes into a lather of suds. There would be a pile of unwashed clothes and a large bar of yellow soap beside him, while those clothes he had already washed were spread out on the tea bushes and rocks to dry and bleach in the sun.

Mother had forbidden him to beat our laundry for he always broke all the buttons, and she was tired of having to replace them after every wash. However he would not change, but when he caught sight of her parasol above the tea bushes, he immediately began scrubbing in the hope that she would not know of his disobedience.

We would cross the river over stepping stones, past islands of soapsuds floating along on the current. As we rounded the bend in the path on the other bank, we would hear again that slap-slap as he returned once more to whacking the dirt out of our clothes.

" There won't be a button left whole!" Mother would sigh, with a despairing laugh.

On our way back, the women would have begun to file back to the factory to have their loads weighed by the tallyman, and their tally sticks notched to record how much they had gathered.

The baskets were then emptied on to cloths spread on the ground, and the women went home for their mid-day meal and siesta. The children who had tormented us on the outward journey, no longer did so in the presence of their mothers.

From time to time we visited the factory, especially when there were guests staying. It was something we regarded as a treat. The factory, the heart of the plantation, was an ugly, long building on three floors, with a corrugated iron roof and many windows, screened with metal lattice to keep out thieves, while ventilating the building. It was situated close to the Lines, facing a large open area, where there were two badminton courts on which the clerks and writers used to play in the late afternoons. Here, too, was a well, source of drinking water for the village. There was always a group of women with their big earthenware pots, gathered there, waiting their turn to draw up the water.

Opposite the main door, a jackfruit tree threw a circle of shade over the bullock carts that rested there between journeys to bring wood to fuel the furnace.

Behind the factory there was a long stack of logs for that purpose. Another of the stories Mother told us on our walks, was of the night the wood stack caught fire. The flames had been visible from the bungalow, and there was a danger that the factory would go up as well.

"The only water within reasonable distance was at the well," she used to tell us, "a chain was formed to pass buckets up to the fire, but it was far too slow, and the water simply evaporated in the heat without reducing the flames at all. It was looking hopeless, and I tried to think of some better way to quench the blaze. Then I remembered that fire can't burn if it's smothered, so I suggested that they threw earth instead of water over it. The men were set to digging up the ground near the fire, and the buckets were used to throw the soil over the woodpile. Luckily that worked, and the fire was put out quite quickly."

She was very proud to think that her presence of mind had saved the factory.

On entering the factory we were instantly aware of two things: the roar of the machines, and the smell of freshly roasted tea. The noise made conversation impossible, but the smell was wonderful!

On the upper floors of the factory were the withering and fermenting rooms, where the fresh leaves were spread on hessian covered shelves and left for several weeks. After fermentation the leaves were sent down a chute to a moving belt on the ground floor. This floor was the exciting one, with pistons hissing as they pounded up and down, sending drive-belts rotating overhead to turn the cogs that worked the machines. A team of women was seated each side of the belt to remove any twigs, stones, or other foreign bodies from the tea. Their hair was bound back with cloths to prevent their long tresses from being caught in the belts. There had been a terrible and unforgettable occasion, when a woman's hair was tangled in one of the drive- belts. Before anyone could stop the machinery, she had been scalped. We always kept well clear of that area, and kept our topees on.

The next stage was the rolling of the leaves. This was what I best liked to watch. Vast, circular vats of brass in which the rollers swung round and round, twisting, not grinding the leaves. The sound of the rollers had a rhythmic throb, like the beating of a gigantic heart. The aroma of tea was mingled with a smell of oil, as the engineers, with long-nozzled cans dripped the lubricant on to the moving parts of the machinery.

The atmosphere was hot, made hotter by the furnaces where after rolling, the green tea was spread on metal trays and loaded into the kiln for seven minutes, or thereabouts. The timing and the temperature was crucial. The man in charge of the kiln was constantly lifting great sheets of heated metal in and out of the oven, tipping the now black tea into a hopper, and reloading the tray. It was a Herculean task, and one that required someone with concentration and a responsible attitude.

In the hopper the tea was sieved and graded into wooden chests lined with tin-foil. The chests were placed on a metal platform which, when switched on, vibrated to settle the contents before they were weighed. When there was a slack moment, Peter and I were allowed to stand on this machine and enjoy the strange sensation of the vibrations.

The room where the tasting took place was near the main door. On a long table a row of white china teapots were lined up beside a row of plain white cups. Tea tasting was always part of the V.A.s duty when they were inspecting the estate, and as part of normal routine Father or one of his assistants would sample every batch before it was despatched.

Peter and I occasionally watched the ceremony, and were inclined to giggle at the sight of grown-ups slurping mouthfuls of scalding fluid and spitting it out again.

Other walks took us along to the dam, or sometimes to a hill which Mother named the 'Green Hill'. It was one of her favourite walks, up a steep, grassy mound, dotted with clumps of citronella grass, whose leaves smelled of lemon, but could cut like razors. White orchids grew here, and the cows were put out to graze. This was where we released the two young hares that had proved too wild to be kept as pets. From the summit there was a vista of jungle-clad hills, shading from blue to purple up towards the High Range, and down towards the Malabar coast.

On a clear day we could glimpse a thin gleam on the horizon: the sea, beyond which were our brother and sister left behind in England. Mother used to say that when she died, it was here that she would like her ashes scattered.

DISCOVERIES

One morning we chose a path we did not often take, behind the bungalow, through a nursery of young bushes to a meadow where sometimes buffalo and bullocks grazed. We were not encouraged to play there because of the presence of the buffaloes.

Sometime before our last leave, one of the great beasts had gored the Sweeper-woman's son. I was taken to see him in the grass hut where he and his mother lived, to give him some of our toys. He lay on his charpoy with a huge white bandage round his stomach, which made him look skinnier and more waifish than ever. Fortunately he survived though the scar remained and his misadventure was a lasting warning to us.

At the upper end of the meadow, a cart track leading from the factory divided to reach the rear of the bungalow and the Estate Office in one direction. The other way followed the contour of the hill past the turning to the Little Bungalow and the pump wheel, towards the dam. At this end there was a shallow well where the native boys sometimes took their buffaloes to drink, sitting on their necks behind the long scimitar-like horns.

A small stream, scarcely more than a rill most of the year, flowed down through the valley to join the upper waters of the larger stream where we liked to paddle.

Also in this upper end of the little valley stood a single tree, its huge trunk gnarled and litchened, its twisted branches like misshapen arms, bearing dull leathery leaves that cast shadows in which the cattle would lie, chewing the cud and shaking the flies out of their eyes. At some time in the past, the tree had been struck by lightning. The top had broken off giving it a rather stunted appearance. It was not a pretty tree and perhaps for that reason we had somehow ignored it.

That morning, however, it caught Peter's attention. He was growing bored with climbing the rose apple and loquat trees in the garden, and was looking for something more challenging. He pleaded with Mother to be allowed to try this one.

"It should be easy once I've got into the branches," he said.

"All right," she said, " Perhaps if there's time on our way back."

We set out down the valley, following the stream. The water was still quite fast-flowing, though by the time the monsoon came, it would have shrunk to a trickle. The dogs, Digger and Mickey ran happily ahead, crossing and recrossing the stream, following scent-trails through the patches of scrub and eta grass on the far side.

As usual as we walked we chattered to Mother and she told us stories of "The Olden Days" when she was a child, and of the adventures of Robert and Ann before they were left behind at school in England. She also told us the latest news from the newspapers, of Gandhi's fasts.

The Tea Planter's Children

"If he dies the British will be blamed and there will be terrible problems," she said. Then someone called Hitler had just been made Chancellor in Germany, and seemed to be another trouble maker.

"That bird Hitler" as Father always referred to him. These two people seemed to cause the grown-ups concern, but were remote to us, in the tranquillity of Arnakal.

At home in England, Mother told us, many people, especially the miners and the ex-soldiers were out of work and starving. They had to line up for something called "The Dole."

" If only," she sighed that morning, "someone could solve the unemployment question."

Looking at the wide green landscape around us, at the white hump-backed cattle and buffaloes grazing with their calves at the end of the valley, I remembered the pictures I had seen in the Madras Mail of men in shabby coats and cloth caps, hunched in the rain as they waited to receive the pittance on which they had to live. At once I thought I knew the answer.

"Why don't they come here?" I said, recalling the tales we had read during our lessons, of the early pioneers who had sailed away to found new colonies when times at home were hard. To my eight-year old eyes, it appeared quite simple. "They could live on the Greenhill, and build their own houses and grow their own food."

Mother smiled down at me. "Yes, perhaps something like that should be done. When you grow up perhaps you will try to do something like that."

We were nearing the end of the valley, so she whistled to call the dogs to her and fastened their leads in case they tried to chase the calves. A previous dog we had had, the

Discoveries

father of Digger, had developed a habit of chasing calves, and unfortunately, he sometimes killed or maimed them, so he had to be destroyed.

We reached the conjunction of the streams and Mother asked if we would like to go on to return home by a different route.

"No, please can we go back the same way." Peter pleaded, "You promised that I could climb that tree."

So we began to retrace our steps. The walk down had been easy, the return journey, as with any expedition from the bungalow, was much harder, not only because it was uphill and we were growing tired, but also because the sun's rays were fiercer and the day was growing steadily hotter. To encourage us to travel faster, Mother found long twigs which we pretended were horses, bestriding them to prance and canter up the hill.

After a little while, Peter complained, " My horse is tired, Mummy. Will you give me a pull, please?"

Mother took his hand, while I fretted and whined because her other hand was holding her parasol, and she could not take mine, so before long we stopped to rest.

Standing by the stream we threw stones into the water to see them splash. Peter, wandering along a little beach looking for suitable stones, called me.

"Eve, quick! Look what I've found."

I ran to where he was scrabbling at the bank.

"Look," he said excitedly, "It's silver."

Sure enough there in the clay of the bank, in a hollow where he had removed a stone, I could see a streak of something with a silvery glint.

"Mummy!" I shouted, "Look what Peter's found."

Peter was clawing at the clay, pulling up handfuls of grass and stones, following the silvery line into the bank, until it became confused with mud and roots.

"I think I've found a silver mine," he said.

"Yes, you're right. It does look just like silver," I agreed excitedly, "Perhaps we'll be rich. Mummy, Mummy! come and look, Peter's found a silver mine."

Mother, laughing at our enthusiasm, came over to look, "It's most probably mica," she said.

We both knew what mica was. It sparkled in every granite rock that protruded from the land all about us.

"It's not mica, I'm sure," I said and Peter agreed, but Mother remained unconvinced. She placated us by suggesting that we look in the Children's Encyclopaedia when we got back to the house. She was more impressed by the clay in which Peter had found his silver mine.

"I didn't know there was any real clay round here. It should come in useful for you to play with." she said. "Now, if you want to spend any time at the tree, we'd better hurry."

We were both thrilled by Peter's discovery, certain that our fortunes were about to be made. We speculated together as to what Father's reaction would be when he knew of the riches that lay nearby just waiting to be mined.

Then we reached the tree. Peter walked all round it to see if there was any point where he could climb up the trunk to reach the branches, but without success. There was, however one small bough that he thought he could reach from Mother's shoulders, and from there it might be possible to reach the main branches.

She lifted him up and he climbed on to her shoulders and stood up. He was just able to grasp the branch and begin to haul himself up. It was obviously a very hard tree to climb, and I was envious of the ape-like agility I so lacked.

While I waited, I wandered round the trunk, looking at the roots that spread across the surface of the ground, twisting serpent-like through the ferns and trampled grass and made a discovery of my own. A darker shadow behind a clump of ferns caught my eye. On pushing them aside I found that the trunk was split and there was an opening into the tree itself. When the lightning had struck, it had burned out the centre of the trunk, leaving it hollow. The split was wide enough for me to squeeze through and wriggle inside, where to my delight I found a space as large as a small room. The floor was carpeted with dead leaves and leaf mould, beneath which twisted roots formed niches and ledges. Above me, the hollow rose upwards, tapering to a blue circle of sky.

I shouted to Peter, thinking he might be able to look down at me from the broken off top of the trunk, but, unknown to me, he had found the tree impossible to climb. There were many dead branches, and those that were sound offered few hand or foot holds, so he had come down again.

Hearing my voice he and Mother began to look round for me, and were puzzled that they could not see me.

"Eve, where are you?" they called.

"Here I am." I said putting my head out through the split. "You'll never believe what I've found."

Peter crawled in to join me. He was impressed. There was plenty of room for both of us

"Why!" said Mother bending down to look in at us, "it's just like the Wendy house in Peter Pan."

We began to play at being Peter Pan and Wendy, but were urged back to the bungalow. It was becoming very hot, and besides, it was time for our lessons.

"You can come back to play here this afternoon, after your rest." Mother promised.

We ran the rest of the way home, full of excitement at the amazing things we had discovered that morning.

After searching through the Children's Encyclopaedia, that Source of all Wisdom, Mother reached the conclusion that what we had found was most probably aluminium.

"It's the most common mineral in the world." She informed us. "However it's very difficult and expensive to smelt. They extract it in Switzerland because they have cheap water power there."

On hearing that, we lost interest, though we wished that someone could find out for certain. Aluminium sounded dull to us, and we did not see how anyone would be able to make a fortune out of something that was used for saucepans. No one, as far as we knew wore aluminium jewellery, or even used it for coins. It was a disappointment but, we consoled ourselves, there was still the tree with its secret hollow that was so perfect for a house. Its discovery heralded many blissful hours to come .

We played there most afternoons from then on. Sometimes I took my dolls down with me, and made mattresses for them of moss and ferns, and prepared feasts for them out of tea-seeds and twigs, and the little yellow and orange flowers that grew on bushes to one side of the tree. The bushes also bore clusters of black berries that we were forbidden to eat for fear of contracting worms

Discoveries

or dysentery. I knew, because I had seen them, that the local children ate them, which proved that they were not poisonous.

Peter and I made plans that when we grew up, we would live in the hollow tree. We thought it was perfectly situated, close to the stream, and near to our parents. The cattle were still grazing in the greener pasture at the lower end of the valley, so we had the meadow to ourselves. We found frogs and grasshoppers in the grass, which sometimes we caught, to be released again after we had looked at them. We hoped, in vain, they would like us enough to stay with us. There were dragonflies with wings as iridescent as the oiled pools, that darted and hovered over the brook, and many butterflies. Happily engrossed, as we were in our own worlds of imagination, the afternoons passed swiftly, until the gong, sounded from our veranda by Francis, called us home for tea.

From the meadow we could see the traffic that travelled along the cart track between the factory and the dam. Bullock and buffalo carts; now and then a lorry or a car; pedestrians, with loads carried on their heads; bicycles. Some of the carts delivered logs to the house and on one, never-to-be-forgotten occasion, after the driver had discharged his load, he invited me to sit beside him and drive the cart. This was an unusual honour. He spoke no English, and my Tamil was fragmentary to say the least, but he managed to show me how to steer the cart by slapping the leathery grey rumps of the buffaloes on the side opposite to the way they were expected to turn. He gave me a stick with which to perform this. Under my guidance the cart veered from side to side along the road, narrowly avoiding hitting the bank or slipping over the edge, to the accompaniment of laughter from the driver and the boy who was with him.

At the end of the cedar grove, he decided that I had gone far enough, and helped me down. I watched him driving away, keeping the cart on a straight course until it vanished round the next bend.

We often saw the tapil coolie bicycling up to the house or the office with the letters and newspapers. Business letters to the Estate office, to the house he carried the weekly letters from our brother and sister and other relatives and friends in England. Sometimes he also brought live chickens from the bazaar at Vandeperiyar, hanging upside down from his handlebars by their bound feet.

We could not have imagined, as we watched the cheerful postman pedalling along towards the house, that one day he might bring a letter that would change our lives forever.

THE FALL

One afternoon during the hot season, Peter decided to see if he could climb the avocado tree that grew below the nursery veranda near the kitchen garden. After failing to climb the hollow tree, he was looking for new challenges. This tree Peter had never climbed nor, as far as we knew, had anyone else. It grew about thirty or forty feet high and somewhat resembled a poplar in that it had a long, straight trunk with many small twigs sprouting from it, while the main canopy and branches began almost halfway up.

We had had our afternoon rest, and the sun was past its zenith, but though it was now cooler outside, the trees' shade was inviting. Mother had told us she had letters to write, so we must entertain ourselves until she was free to take us for a walk with the dogs.

Peter, though two years my junior, was far better at climbing than I was. I suffered from a fear of heights, and a tendency to get my feet wedged in the angles where branches forked, and often had to be rescued. However, the rose-apple tree by the garage was easy to climb with conveniently spaced branches and places where I could perch to look out at the world from on high.

Peter, agile as a monkey and as fearless of heights, was bored with the rose-apple and with the loquat trees that grew in that part of the garden, and having failed to climb the hollow tree, was in the mood for something more challenging, which the tree on the nursery lawn certainly was.

"Wave when you get to the top," I said as we went our separate ways. I would be able to see the top of the tree across the roof of the bungalow when I was up in the rose-apple.

Mother came out to see what we were doing, coming first to me as I was the nearest. She stayed to watch as I began my ascent. It had been she who had taught us to climb as soon as we were able. As a small girl in Oxfordshire, in the 1890s she had been a champion climber, out-climbing most of the village boys, scaling the local elms to collect eggs from the rookeries.

She had dinned into us the three cardinal rules of climbing: first, to test every hand or foothold before transferring our weight to it; second, to watch for dead branches, and third, never to look down.

She was reassured that I was safe where I was, because I was so familiar with the tree.

"I'd better go and see how Peter's getting on," she said, "I don't suppose he'll be able to get up that tree, the branches are too high."

I watched her walk away towards the far side of the bungalow and not long afterwards saw her coming back.

"I told Peter I'd better not stay," she said, "I'll just make him nervous and distract him, so he'll be more likely to have an accident. I'm going in to write to Robert and Ann. Be careful, won't you, darling?"

It was characteristic of her that she did not stop Peter from tackling an untested and difficult climb, in spite of her own nervousness.

I managed to scramble a good way up the rose-apple tree, and sat astride a branch, my back to the trunk. From where I sat I could see the top of Peter's tree. Presently his head emerged, a dark shape silhouetted amongst the leaves. I recognised him more by his movement than by shape. His head rose through the branches until I could see his whole body. He was at the top of the tree, amongst the smallest boughs.

"Cooee!" I called, "Peter! I can see you."

He turned towards me and waved. I waved back, envious in the knowledge that I would never find the courage to emulate his prowess.

"Cooee!" He shouted back, "I can see for miles and miles, it's wonderful. I can see right to the dam."

I stood up on the bough on which I had been sitting and holding on to a branch above my head, I began to make it swing up and down. Across the bungalow I saw Peter begin to copy me and heard him laugh as he pushed the branches up and down more and more violently, bouncing up and down at the top of his tree. He waved again.

It was then I heard a sharp report like a shot and Peter vanished from my view. The sound of his shriek reached me as I was already trying to scramble out of the rose-apple tree. Knowing what must have happened, I began to shout at the top of my voice.

"Mummy! Mummy! Quick! Help, help! Peter's fallen. Mummy, help!"

Inevitably one of my sandals was jammed fast in a fork, trapping me.

Mother came out on to the veranda steps. "What's the matter, Eve? Are you all right, darling?"

"It's Peter. Quick! He's fallen out of the tree."

She turned and ran, while I struggled to free myself. With shaking fingers, at last I managed to undo the buckle and pull my foot out of my sandal. I jumped to the ground and ran lopsidedly to the nursery lawn, where I found Mother and Kunichin standing beside Peter who lay spread-eagled on the ground under the tree. Pieces of dead branch were scattered around him. He appeared unconscious.

A moment later he opened his eyes but was obviously shocked and badly winded by the fall. Anxiously, Mother was looking to see how badly he was hurt.

"Look, what's that on his leg?" I said, pointing to a dark object that seemed to protrude from his thigh just below his shorts.

Mother bent down and pulled out a thick piece of stick that was embedded in his leg. Blood began to spurt and a huge swelling rose like an inflating balloon.

"Kunichin," Mother said, maintaining a calm and collected appearance in spite of the alarm she must have been experiencing. "Kunichin, go and find Totemcurran and get the gate from the kitchen garden. We need something to carry him up to the house. We must be very

The Fall

careful how we move him until we know if he's broken anything."

At this moment Father arrived and came across to see what we were looking at.

"Good God!" was all he said when he saw Peter, and pulling out his handkerchief, he made a tourniquet on Peter's leg to stop the flow of blood.

Francis too, was hovering in the background, looking distressed at the sight of Peter's prostrate body.

So far Peter had not spoken but he was beginning to show signs that he was awake.

"How far did you fall, darling?" Mother asked.

"From the top." He said in a faint voice. "I grabbed a branch to save myself, but I couldn't hold on."

Kunichin came back with the gardener and the gate. With Mother's help Peter was eased carefully on to this makeshift stretcher and carried into the house.

"We must get Dr Miller to look at him." Father said, "I'll go and fetch him, shall I, Mam?" He looked down at me as I stood, terrified, staring at the limp form of my little brother with his unnaturally pale face and the great bulge at the top of his leg. I was afraid he was going to die.

"Why don't you come with me, Eve?" Father asked.

I nodded, glad of something to do. Mother was busy stanching the wound, swabbing it with a solution of permanganate of potash and warm water, one of her stock remedies.

As we drove towards Dr Miller's home, my father questioned me about what we had been doing.

"How far up the tree had he got?" he asked.

I was sitting hunched up on the front seat beside him, trying to will the car to cover the distance quickly.

"To the very top." I said. "He was waving to me across the roof."

"Then he must have fallen at least thirty feet," said my father. "Lucky he managed to catch hold of that branch. It must have saved his life."

He fell silent, and for the rest of the journey we did not speak. Both of us were shaken by the accident, and anxious to know how badly Peter was injured. He had been too stunned to cry. Silently I began to bargain with God.

"Please God, let Peter be all right. Please let him not be badly hurt. I promise to be good. Please don't let him die, God, and I'll never quarrel with him or tease him again, I promise, God." and so on.

When we returned with Dr Miller, Peter was still pale, but more aware of what was going on. He complained that his leg hurt and his right arm. The doctor examined him closely, rolling him over with care to make sure he had not injured his spine, testing his reflexes, and shining a torch into his eyes.

"You're a very lucky laddie," he said, and turned to Mother. "He hasn't damaged his back, though, of course there are plenty of bruises. He has, however, broken his left femur. I don't think it is a complete fracture, most likely what is known as a greenstick fracture. With a child, the bones are more pliable and tend to crack rather than fracture. He'll be all right in a week or so. We'd better give him some splints to hold it straight."

Slats from a wooden crate were padded with cotton wool and bound with strips of sheet ready to be bandaged

The Fall

to Peter's leg. But first his leg had to be pulled out to make sure it was straight.

This was the worst part as it involved Dr Miller having a tug-of-war with Peter's leg, with one foot placed in his groin. That was the first time Peter made any sort of fuss. At first his leg had been numb as injuries often are, but by now all feeling had returned, and with the wound in his thigh, it must have been agonising for him. Mother had given him an aspirin to lessen the pain, but he had had no other anaesthetic. Dr Miller attempted to give him chloroform, but by then Peter was so terrified that he threw the mask across the room. I was removed at this point, and when I returned the splints were tied in place, though the wound had made this difficult. However, it was managed somehow.

Peter complained again about the pain in his arm.

"I think that was sprained when you caught hold of that branch," Dr Miller said," That will get better with a bit of rest. Give him some more aspirin," he told Mother, "it might help him to sleep tonight. You can give him two aspirin every four hours or so. I'll come and look at him again tomorrow."

We all felt a great sense of relief that Peter had not been more badly injured, but he slept badly that night, and I awoke once or twice to the flickering light of a candle as Mother came to see to him. His leg throbbed and he found it difficult to find a position to ease his aching bruises. I heard him crying quietly in the dark.

As the days passed he grew stronger and was able to joke about his accident. The wound in his leg was a problem, for it was deep and took a while to close. After a couple of weeks, Dr Miller tried to get him to test his weight on his leg, but it was so painful that Peter could not do it. The doctor was puzzled by this. By now the bone should have knitted, he thought, and he should have been able to walk on it again.

"I think he ought to have it X-rayed," he said, "to make sure it is setting as it should."

"What is an X-ray?" we asked, and it was explained to us that it was a special kind of light that could shine right through a body and show up all the bones. We laughed a good deal over the ideas that this information stimulated. We had discovered for ourselves that our hands, when held over a lighted torch, would glow red, with the bones of our fingers darker red shadows within the crimson flesh. The idea that you could become invisible except for your skeleton was food for all sorts of fantasies.

There was only one place where Peter could be X-rayed, and that was the hospital at Nargacoil where, only a few months previously I had had my tonsils removed. An ambulance was booked to transport Peter. Mother and I accompanied him. He was placed on a narrow berth on one side, and his broken leg fastened by the foot to the ceiling, so that he had to travel the whole journey with one foot in the air. Mother and I sat in the back of the ambulance with him, so we could look after him on the long drive. And what a long drive it was! We dozed, played card games and Mother read to us to pass the time. As it was the hot season and we were travelling through the day, the ambulance was like an oven. There were stops for refreshment on the way.

We had no appetite in the heat, but we were given green coconuts in their husks with the tops cut off. The milk, drunk through a straw, was deliciously cool and

The Fall

creamy. It was the best treat we could have had. We also unhooked Peter's leg from the ceiling, as he was finding it far more uncomfortable than when it was laid flat.

Since this was our second visit to the hospital, we did not feel any strangeness on our arrival. We were even given the room we had had before, on the upper floor.

But there were differences of which we rapidly became aware. Naturally the patients who had befriended us then had left. Nurse Wolf, who had been my nurse, now had another patient to take care of, and had little time to make a fuss of me.

She had made me a beautiful dress of blue silk, sprigged with rosebuds, and matching slip and knickers which I could only wear for best occasions but would have worn every day had it been allowed. So I was hurt when I rushed up to her, only to have her excuse herself to go to her new charge.

In addition, one of the doctors we had got to know, had left to work in a leper colony. At that time, this meant that he, himself, would run a high risk of becoming infected.

Above all, the weather was different. It had been warmer than we were accustomed to, on that last visit, but not unbearably so, and the nights were cool. Now the days were stifling, in spite of a constant wind that blew night and day, for, hot and dry, it buffeted and nagged in a way that made everyone tired and irritable. Mosquitoes came in through the broken mesh of the fly-screens. Though we were safe under our mosquito nets at night, during the day, in spite of liberal applications of citronella oil, they bit us unmercifully.

Peter's and my beds were placed on the veranda for coolness but I think it did not make much difference and exposed us to the wind.

Peter's X-ray showed that the break in his femur had healed and the pain was mainly due to the wound, where the piece of wood had pierced the muscle and caused lesions as it healed. However, in spite of Dr Miller's attempt to stretch his leg before putting on the splints, it had set slightly crookedly, and was , in consequence, a little shorter than the other.

Dr Noble, brisk and dapper as I remembered him, discussed his plans with our mother.

"We'll try traction. It's possible we can straighten the leg, since he's young and the bones are still growing. We'll find a splint for him and put a weight on his foot to pull it out."

It soon became clear that more discomfort was in store for poor Peter. Since, at that time he was a small and skinny six-year-old, the hospital had no metal splints small enough to fit him. He was put into an iron splint, the smallest they had but huge on Peter, and, by means of sticking plaster along his leg, fastened a large brick that hung over the end of his bed. The weight of it dragged him down the bed, and he had frequently to be pulled back on to his pillows.

His nurse was a middle-aged woman, caring in her way, but she had been trained to be cruel to be kind. When it was time to wash him and change his dressings, she insisted that it was better to strip off the sticking plaster quickly, rather that spend time soaking it. Peter's arms and legs were covered with downy fair hair, which I had often drawn attention to during our quarrels, when

The Fall

I compared him to a monkey. This did not make it any easier when pulling off the plaster, and his skin became raw in places.

Since we were likely to be there for sometime, Mother decided to have a minor gynaecological operation that she evidently had needed for some time, so she was confined to bed as well, and was unable to do much to help Peter.

After about a week, Dr Noble decided that the slight distortion of his leg was not worth the discomfort Peter suffering and removed the splint. Mother let him come into her bed with her during the day, which comforted him. He was looked on as a little hero because he complained so little.

"You're a tough little chap, aren't you?" said Dr Noble when he was examining him one day.

"Yes. Look at my forceps!" Peter replied, doubling up his fists to show off the two small lumps that were his biceps.

As the only able-bodied member of the family, the time dragged for me. I passed the days reading and drawing. I was beginning to experiment with drawings of animals, but still had difficulty in working out which way their legs bent. I was listless and uncomfortable in the heat, as I scratched at my mosquito bites.

The incessant wind blew directly on to the veranda, setting the curtains flapping and creating a constant flutter of leaves and creaking branches, whistling through the fly-screen, blowing light objects across the veranda. There were intermissions when it was merely hot, but they never seemed to last long.

Now and then something would happen to enliven the boredom. One day, amid the sound of bells and gongs, a parade passed along the road outside the hospital compound, which I could see from our veranda. It was led by a white elephant, fully caparisoned, accompanied by bobbing parasols of scarlet and gold silk with silver fringes. When it passed from view into the dusty distance, I made a drawing of it, the first elephant I had ever seen.

The sunbirds in the creeper that draped the veranda pillars had built a nest, a beautiful ovoid of woven grass with a small round hole through which they flew in and out to feed their chicks. I watched them every day until I thought the last chick had gone, then I climbed up and broke off the creepers to which it was attached and lifted it down.

To my dismay a tiny egg fell out and smashed at my feet. No use to replace the nest now, the birds would never return I knew, so when we went back to Arnakal, I took it with me.

Father drove down to visit us, to see how Peter and Mother were, and to leave the car for us when we came home. It would have been difficult for Peter to get on or off the train, even though he was beginning to learn to get about on crutches. Like the splint, these, too, were rather too big for him.

At last he and Mother were well enough to leave. We spent a day or two at Kovalum and along the coast at the southern- most tip of India, paddling and collecting shells. Peter hopped along happily through the surf. The restless wind that had tormented us in Nargacoil, was a refreshing breeze by the sea. The mosquito bites that we had scratched raw, were not healed by the salt water as we had hoped, but they were cooled and soothed a little.

The Fall

There were few other people staying in the hotel at that time, but there was an elderly couple, the Resident and his wife, who befriended us. On one occasion, as we were walking along the beach with them at low tide, the old man peered into a rock pool.

"There's an octopus in there." He said, and began to poke about under an over-hanging rock with the stick he used for walking until something seemed to grip it. He gave the stick a hefty tug and a pink, gelatinous lump came to the surface, the octopus. The old man landed it on the sand. It let go of the stick and ran the few feet that lay between it and the surf, to disappear into the waves, leaving us staring after it in amazement that it could actually move across the ground using it's tentacles as legs. Something we could never have imagined.

After Kovalum, there was another stop at Trivandrum to visit our parents' friends, and for a chance to revisit the zoo. Here as at the hospital, there had been changes. The giraffes greeted us again by bending their long necks over the railings to take our offerings of leaves and grass from our hands; and the gibbons still performed their graceful acrobatics along their cages, and swung on their extraordinarily long arms. But the lion cubs seemed almost full-grown, and of a pair of zebras, only one remained, the male having been kicked to death by the mare.

At the house, the punka wallah had to work harder than ever in the heat, but in the dawn, when we awoke each day, the garden was a paradise of coolness and filled with bird-song. Then as the sun rose the heat and dust returned, enervating and exhausting. We longed for Arnakal and the coolness of the hills.

It was to be a long and tiring drive back up the ghat along the narrow winding road. We stopped frequently for either Peter or me to be sick, but as we climbed the air grew cooler and fresher. Apart from the steepness of the gradient our rate of progress was further impeded by the need to pull into the side to allow lorries , bullock-carts and herds of cattle to pass.

During one of these pauses, Mother failed to notice a storm drain and the rear wheel slipped over the edge. There was a bump, the car tilted sharply sideways and no matter how much she revved the engine, it would not move. The lorry, which had caused our mishap, had rattled on out of sight. At that moment there was no one else to be seen, not even a bullock-cart. We all got out of the car. Peter, who by this time could manage with one crutch, hopped round like a miniature Long John Silver.

Presently a bullock-cart rounded the bend, coming up hill. The driver saw our predicament and got down to see if he could help, leaving his cart blocking the road.

Another cart appeared from the opposite direction. The driver sat looking annoyed but did not offer to help. A lorry now drew up behind the first cart, and in no time at all there was a jam of carts and lorries in both directions. Several men got out of their vehicles and conferred as to the best way to tackle the task of putting the car back on the road. In the end they lifted it out bodily.

After Mother had distributed her change amongst those who had helped us, we all got back into the car. It took sometime to ease our way past the long line of waiting carts and flocks of goats that by then stretched almost a quarter of a mile, and it must have taken hours

The Fall

for the two lines of traffic to free themselves from the jam.

At last we began to recognise landmarks as we neared Peermade district and the road to Arnakal.

Peter's leg improved rapidly once we were home again. The swelling on his thigh took several months to disappear but it was not long before he could walk without limping.

The chief mementoes we brought back from Nagacoil were the mosquito bites, which festered where we had scratched them, and were slow to heal. Mother bathed them with permanganate and bandaged them with lint and strips of sheet. These were forever coming undone and sliding down our legs or arms, but in the end the sores healed and the whole adventure became a memory. However, Peter did not try to climb that tree again.

CONCERNING ELEPHANTS

Although the elephant is often used to symbolise India, Peter and I had never seen a live one, except in pictures, until that day while we were staying at the hospital in Nagacoil, when we had heard a great commotion beyond the hospital compound. Gongs and drums and bells and people shouting. In the distance we had glimpsed thronging crowds and the big fringed sunshades that were held over the heads of important personages. In their midst, as I described in the previous chapter, an elephant, fully caparisoned with bright cloths and golden chains, a mahout seated behind its head, a howdah on its back. Perhaps it was bearing the Maharaja, or some other dignitary, to a festival. It moved slowly, ponderously, through the throng amid clouds of dust. From where I stood on our first floor veranda, distant though I was, I saw, flapping slowly to and fro to drive the flies away from its eyes, ears that were not the expected grey, but mottled pink. The trunk and legs beneath the cloths and tassels with which it was hung, were also pale. It was not just an elephant, but a white elephant, rare and sacred.

Concerning Elephants

I felt sorry for it, for I thought the creature looked unhappy and unhealthy.

I stood at the rail and stared after the procession until it became a silhouette on the horizon, then a hump-backed blob, which vanished into the dusty haze and afterwards I made a drawing of my first elephant. It had been an exciting incident in a rather tedious period, for the weather had been hot and windy, and, with both Peter and Mother confined to bed, there was little to keep me amused during the weeks of our stay.

Some months later, just after the monsoon, which had been wetter than usual that year, Peter and I were walking back from Munjamully with Mother.

"Look, children," she said, pointing across the valley to the opposite hillside. "There are the elephants. I heard they were up this way."

In the distance, across the scrubby jungle, we saw grey shapes that looked like boulders rising out of the eta grass until they moved. It was a family group of adults and calves of various ages, browsing on the vegetation as they roamed along the hillside.

"I want to see them nearer," said Peter. "Will they come to our bungalow?"

"I hope not," Mother said, "they do a lot of damage. The villagers get very angry because they knock down their houses and walk all over their crops, but no one is allowed to touch them."

The Maharaja had forbidden anyone to harm the elephants in any way, with the result that they did as they liked. There was a tradition that the Rajah's dynasty would end if there were no elephants, and this contributed to his affection for them.

The Tea Planter's Children

A few nights later they passed through the estate near the factory, tearing up tea bushes as they went and breaking down the shade trees. Where high banks bordered the roads, they used them as scrapers, rubbing their sides up and down against the rough embankments until they crumbled in minor landslides. Huge and clumsy, they gambolled like playful giants, leaving trails of wreckage behind them.

A favourite pastime of the young elephants was to climb a steep slope and slither down the other side, creating long scars in the terraces of tea. Because they were protected, they had no fear of humans. One local planter awoke in the night to find himself face to face, as it were, with the waving trunk of an elephant that had put its head through his bedroom window.

Everywhere the conversation was about elephants. Our neighbour from the Little Bungalow, the junior assistant, Mr Wilshaw, called round one morning in a state of great excitement.

As he sipped a whisky-and-soda he recounted to our parents his adventures of the previous evening. He had set out, he said, to spend the evening with the Gilbeys who lived at Mount, some miles beyond the dam, through wild jungly country. The road was rough and rocky, rutted by the wheels of bullock-carts, as most roads became during the rainy season, and wound and twisted along the contours of the hills. He was riding his ancient motorcycle, notorious for its tendency to break down.

"Just as I was coming to a blind turn," he told us, "what happened but my ruddy lights went out. I came round the bend and there right in front was this great black shape. I jammed on my brakes and my engine stalled. For a moment I wondered if I'd lost my bearings and gone off the road among the rocks, but then I realised... well, I smelt it actually...elephant! I didn't know what to do. The moon was beginning to rise so it wasn't completely dark and I could make out another huge one to my right and beyond that, several more with calves amongst them.

It was a long way back here, and Doris and Gilly were expecting me. They'd be worried if I just didn't turn up, so I took a chance and began to walk, very slowly and quietly through them. My God! Was I scared!"

Fortunately, in spite of there being calves with them, the herd was not alarmed by him. They were dozing and ruminating by the edge of the jungle.

He walked slowly, wheeling his machine, giving them as wide a berth as he could, until he managed to find the road again. Had not his lights failed and his engine stalled, the story that night might easily have been a tragedy, for the creatures would almost certainly have panicked. Elephants were known to dislike the sound of motorbikes and attack them.

Once he was well clear of the herd he tried to restart his motor. Luck was still with him, he managed to get it going again and reached the Gilbeys shaken and in urgent need of a stiff drink. Without much difficulty he was persuaded to stay the night there.

In the morning, when he returned the way he had come, to his relief, the herd had moved away.

We did not see the elephants again. They moved slowly out of the district, leaving a trail of destruction behind them which gradually healed until we were left with only the memory of those moving boulders on that distant hillside, and the stories which became legends.

The Tea Planter's Children

One of the stories which people remembered from the past, was of the planter who unwisely had a bungalow built on an elephant path. A ditch was dug round the site, fires were lit at night, drums beaten, but every night a herd of the great beasts surrounded it, trumpeting their disapproval.

On completion, the planter moved in, but still, in spite of the fires, which were still kept alight, the herd continued nightly to trumpet their anger. Guns were fired to drive them away but to no avail. Finally, the planter gave in and moved away. The next day all that remained of the bungalow was a chimney, rising out of the ruins. The next night even that was flattened.

At Christmas the Rice Merchant, the richest man in the district, gave us a wonderful collection of clockwork toys. As usual his more lavish gifts were declined, but the toys were accepted for us. Made of pink celluloid, they formed a circus. There were two elephants, one that nodded its head as it rolled along; the other was seated and clapped a pair of cymbals. They had smiling mouths and eyes, and accoutrements painted in bright colours. There was also a dancing bear, a monkey that beat a drum, a nodding dog and a tiger. Garish as they were, more reminiscent of the highly coloured statues and pictures of Ganesh, the elephant god we saw in the bazaar in Vandiperiyar, than the grey, rock-like shapes on the hillside, or the distant white elephant of the procession. However, they gave us a great deal more entertainment.

THE MONSOON

Peter falling from a tree and breaking his leg interrupted our preoccupation with the hollow tree. The weather was at its hottest, so that our weeks in the Plains at Nargacoil Hospital were uncomfortable and debilitating. By the time we returned home, the monsoon was approaching. Peter, still quite lame, hopped about with the help of a stick, but found it difficult to walk very far or over rough ground, so I went alone to visit the tree.

The meadow was baked dry and the stream was greatly reduced, but I had plans to make a garden amongst the roots of the tree. Mother had been thinning out some plants,(the same species of lily as the ones that failed to flower in my garden under the rose-apple tree,) and gave me some of the plants. Undeterred by my previous lack of success, I borrowed a trowel and took the bulbs down to the hollow tree. It turned out to be a similar experience to my attempt to bury the kittens, though the result was less horrific! The ground was much too hard to make much impression on it, but I managed to scrape out some shallow trenches amongst the grey, serpentine roots that protruded from the ground. I pressed the lilies into them, and scratched up enough soil to cover them, but it was dust-dry and powdery, so, taking an empty cigarette tin,(a most useful tool for many purposes,) I fetched water from the stream, as I knew I should when putting in new plants. The water was rather oily and difficult to scoop out of the tiny trickle the stream had shrunk to, but it wetted the ground a little, although it also washed some of the earth off the plants. I hoped that when the monsoon began, the bulbs would settle and root themselves, so that when the weather improved, they would flower. I pictured the carpet of blossom that would greet me after the rains!

That year the monsoon was exceptionally heavy. The Madras Mail reported floods everywhere. Thunderstorms and high winds uprooted huge trees and roads were frequently blocked. We heard that Dr Miller's car had been crushed by a falling tree as he was driving back from visiting a patient. He was concussed for an hour or two, but came to and, after being rescued by someone who came across the accident, carried on as usual, though he did admit to a severe headache.

Confined to the bungalow for days on end, we invented games as we watched the white spurts of water thrown up as the raindrops splashed down on the flooded drive.

"They look like ducks diving." Said Peter.

We admired the lightning as it forked across the clouds above the surrounding hills, which reverberated to the sound of thunder. "God's horses are galloping," we told each other. Thunderstorms were as exciting as fireworks displays to us, safe, as we thought, in the bungalow, though the rain was beating on the roof and deluging down the gutters. The cart-drivers wore palm-leaf matting to shield them from the rain. The clerks and writers from the office, and the kanganies carried large black umbrellas. On one occasion, as Mother drove us to visit Munjamully in a hailstorm, we saw a man turn his umbrella upside-down to catch the lumps of falling ice. We thought that probably he wanted to take them home to his family, but we knew that the heat meant that they would melt too fast for that to be possible.

To keep us occupied during the long days when we could not go outside, Mother thought up schemes to amuse us. As no guests were expected, we were allowed to play in one of the spare rooms. As well as beds, it was furnished with a table and chairs.

She found us a huge old cotton carpet which, with difficulty, we managed to drape over the table to make a den. It was folded double and we found that we could crawl between the layers, through secret passages along the 'walls', and invented stories which we acted out as we played.

Remembering the clay we had found, Mother sent Totemcurran, during a break in the rain, to collect a bucketful for us. It was excellent clay, though slightly sandy, and ideal for modelling. We already had plasticine and in addition sometimes we were given flour-and-water dough to play with. The dough was difficult to shape into anything other than snakes or roughly shaped lumps that, when a thumb was pressed into them, formed a crude cup shape. These could be baked hard if Muttu had room in the oven. The plasticine, while more malleable, could not be baked, and the colours would merge into each other no matter how we tried to keep them separate, and became a dreary greyish brown.

The clay had some of the qualities of both these materials, and occasionally Muttu would agree to put our creations into the oven after he had finished cooking. We made little 'thumb pots' as with the dough, but they were easier to shape. There were also numerous snakes, of course, rolled out between our palms, and coiled into cobras with heads raised threateningly, or into bowls or baskets. We became engrossed for hours at a time, exploring the possibilities of the clay.

One wet day Peter and I invented a wonderful game. It began with a quarrel.

We frequently squabbled at this time, especially when we could not go out of doors. Since we had to rely solely on each other for companionship most of the time, it was not surprising that, fond though we were of each other, from time to time we got on each other's nerves. In fine weather there was plenty of space to avoid each other when we felt the need. However, we had moods when it amused us to taunt each other until one of us would become maddened and, losing their temper, would attack. It could begin with something as innocent as a competition to see who could pull the most hideous grimace. This almost always roused us to fury. Watching monkeys in zoos, I have noticed similar behaviour.

On this occasion it had come about because I had decided to act as if I was more grown-up by reason of my age. I was still influenced by the memory of Peggy's visit two years before, when she had declared with absolute confidence that fairies did not exist. At the time, Peter and I had loyally stood by our beliefs because we could not bear to think of a world without magic. But the seeds of doubt had been sown, and now wishing to copy Peggy's sophistication, I stated that fairies were untrue.

Peter stuck manfully to his opinion, (which until that moment I had shared,) that just because they were invisible to human eyes, it did not mean that they did not exist.

A furious battle followed. Peter rushed to attack me, fists clenched, screaming with rage. "They are true! They are true!"

I fled, knowing, from experience that I usually lost physical fights with Peter. We ran from room to room, taking care to keep away from where our parents might be. Peter was gaining on me as we dodged round the furniture in the guest bedrooms. I saw that I was cornered. By this time I was beginning to realise that I really did not want to renounce my belief in fairies, but at the same time I was not willing to admit I was wrong. I thought fast.

"Anyway," I said, still maintaining my position of superiority, and dodging Peter's fists, "I should know, because I'm the Queen of the Fairies."

"What?" shouted Peter, confused by what I had said, "Of course you're not!"

"Yes I am," I answered calmly, "I'm married to the Fairy King."

"Don't be stupid. Of course you're not. How could you be?"

I had stopped him from hitting me, and though he was still very angry, I could see his temper cooling.

"In the middle of the night, when you're fast asleep, I go to Fairyland." I was inventing as fast as I could, and the ideas that were coming into my head were fascinating me.

"I thought you said fairies weren't true," Peter protested, but I could see the idea was catching on with him.

"Never mind that," I said dismissively, "I really am the Queen."

"What's the King called, then?"

"William." I said, seizing on the first name that came to mind, "William Wilson."

"Well, you're wrong, because I'm the King." said Peter, determined to have a part in this fantasy.

"All right. But you must be King of a different part of Fairyland. William lives up in the sky, in Upperland. Where do you live?"

"Under the dam," he said after a moments thought, "in Lowerland."

That was the beginning and we went on to invent our adventures in Upper and Lowerland. We named our children, and thought up the means by which our kingdoms could be reached. Upperland, I decided, was reached by standing in the middle of the lawn outside our bedroom veranda and calling out a magic word, whereon William Wilson would lower a staircase, which I would mount as he wound it up behind me.

Later I changed this to a pony on which I galloped upwards as the road was rolled up again. I needed to ride fast to avoid being rolled up inside it.

The descent to Lowerland was through a secret door in the wall of the dam, also opened by a magic password. The entrance led to a long passage that descended into the depths of the earth, where his wife, Morning Glory awaited him.

The fantasy continued from then on. My declared disbelief in fairies was not mentioned again as we added almost every day to our imaginary worlds. We planned State Visits it each other's realms, describing the carriages and horses, the provisions we were taking, and our retinue. Our imaginings held very little of the ethereal, but I began to half believe that William Wilson really existed somewhere the other side of my dreams. I longed to recall the magic word that would bring the staircase down to me. Waking at night, I would try to find the courage to go out alone into the garden to see if I was able to remember it and have my fantasy come true. But, of course I knew that I could not, and in any case the garden seemed an eerie place in the starlight, when even the sounds were different from those of daytime.

On days when the rain eased from torrential to showery we would put on our raincoats and wellingtons and splash out for a walk with the dogs, taking the drier routes along the road to the dam, or Munjamully, or through the village. The lower part of the meadow below the bungalow, was flooded, and the cattle had moved up near the hollow tree so we did not venture there.

As the weather improved, and the grass began to dry, the streams returned to their normal channels and the cattle returned to the damp pasture in the valley, we began to play by the tree again. Peter's leg was completely healed by now, though he was left with a slight bulge on his thigh where the break had been. We still needed to wear wellingtons for the grass had grown long and was full of leeches. They would cling to the grass stalks, waving their heads about as they tasted the air for their prey. Even when wearing our boots, we would frequently feel a need to scratch our legs, only to come into contact with a rubbery grey blob clinging to us, rapidly swelling and reddening with our blood. Sometimes we could make them release their hold by rolling them to and fro, but more usually a lighted cigarette or a burning match had to be applied before they would let go. If we tried to drag them off, there was a danger that they would break leaving their mouth-parts affixed to our flesh where they were likely to fester.

We did not like leeches. There were many stories of travellers dying in the jungle drained of blood by leeches. However, having grown up aware of their nasty parasitic ways, we accepted them as an unpleasant part of our lives.

When I went back to visit the tree, there was a disappointment in store for me. I had hoped to find a garden there, where I had tried to plant the lilies, but far from being greeted by a carpet of flowers that had rooted themselves during the wet season, the rain had washed the soil away, and now the bulbs lay strewn about, crushed and broken by the hooves of the cattle that had sheltered under the tree. It was another disillusionment, but I forgot my disappointment as I set about looking for dry moss and ferns to cushion the floor of the hollow.

At about this time the Visitng Agents (V.As) came to stay. This was a regular occurrence from time to time. Usually they were friendly to us children, and once one of them brought his twenty year old daughter with him. We helped Mother to entertain her while her father was busy with estate matters. That it was she who insisted on drowning the baby rats I was trying to rescue, did not make me dislike her for long. Later she had sent me a beautiful French doll, which I named 'Poppy'.

This time there were two V.A.s both of whom we knew from previous visits. Mr Sylvester, a small brisk man, with horn-rimmed spectacles, who was uninterested in children and usually ignored us, and Mr Barker, a friendlier man, whose name we found hilarious. We began to call Digger 'Mr Barker' when, as was his habit, he began barking at the visitors, but we took care not to do so in Mr Barker's hearing.

The V.A.s spent the days at the factory and on the Estate with Father. They also seemed to spend a lot of time with Mr Gowan. Their presence made little difference to the routines of our lives. We were not to know that, in fact, they were to be responsible for altering them completely.

While the guests were staying, Peter and I were still engrossed in playing down by the hollow tree. Then one afternoon as I played by the tree and Peter was busy by the stream, he called to me: "Eve, come here, quickly. Look what I've found."

I ran to where he was crouched on the bank, staring down into the water. Looking to see what he thought was so interesting, to my amazement I saw what could only be a crab, resting on the sandy floor of the brook. Brownish, with stiff-looking legs and a pair of pincers. The shell was about two inches across, beneath which its protuberant eyes shifted from side to side and upwards towards us. We sat motionless, fascinated.

"I thought crabs lived in the sea." I whispered.

"Aren't there land crabs?" asked Peter. We decided to ask Mother.

Picking up a twig, Peter held it close to the crab's claws. It seized it, and Peter tried to pull it out of the water, but it let go and scuttled sideways under the bank, stirring up a cloud of mud. He poked about under the bank to see if he could chase the creature out again, but only succeeded in making the water too muddy for us to be able to make out anything that might be hidden there. After waiting several minutes to see if the mud would settle, we got bored and went away to do something else.

A little later I heard Peter call me again. "Quick! There's another one here."

This time he was standing by the well. The water was dark, the bottom full of rotting leaves deposited by the monsoon storms. At first I could see nothing but the dark shapes of dead leaves, then realised that something I had taken for a large leaf, was in fact a shell. I had no doubt about what sort of shell it was, but this was much larger that that of the crab in the stream, a good nine inches across. I watched the claws moving slowly to and fro in front of it. It seemed to us unnatural and sinister, this invasion of out peaceful meadow by creatures that ought to belong to a different environment.

"How did they get here?" I said.

"Perhaps they've always been here." Peter suggested.

"But why haven't we seen them before?" I wanted to know.

"The tree has been here a long time, but we didn't notice it until recently. We just never played down here." Peter reasoned.

I had to agree. "But we've paddled in the stream. What if they had pinched our toes? Ugh!"

The Monsoon

That evening over our boiled eggs and cocoa at supper, we told Mother about the crabs and questioned how they had got there.

"Probably they were washed down by the rain storms." She suggested. That sounded likely, the monsoon was only just over, but it did not explain from whence they were washed down.

That night, as I lay safely tucked up inside the mosquito net, I listened as so often I did, to the familiar sounds of the house in the evening. Because we did not like the dark, a lamp was placed beside the water filter on the table outside our room, and the door left ajar, so that a shaft of golden light shone across the floor. A dinner party was in progress to entertain the V.A.s. I could hear the chink of silver and glass, the soft rustle of Francis or Kunichin's dhoti and the padding of their sandalled feet as they hurried to and fro from the kitchen; Father's voice rising above the blur of conversation to call: "Boy!" and the sudden burst of sound as the door was opened, that reduced again as it closed, and Mother's laugh, clear and unmistakable amid all the other sounds.

Enclosed though I was, within all these familiar sounds, with the reassurance of the dim lamplight, still I lay awake, thinking over the day's events. I felt uneasy about the arrival of the crabs. We had seen only two, but how many more might be hiding there?

I lay awake for what seemed like a long time. I could hear by Peter's rhythmic breathing that he was asleep, and tried to turn my thoughts to William Wilson and what might be going on in Upperland, but they kept returning to the crabs. I knew that tomorrow we would have to go back to see if they were still there.

The Tea Planter's Children

Next morning we went straight to the stream to find the first crab where we had seen it before, looking up at us through the water with its unblinking eyes on their stalks. A worm had fallen into the stream higher up, and was being washed towards the crab. As we watched, it lunged forward with surprising agility, and seized the worm with one claw. There it writhed and struggled to get free, but the crab began to fold it, bit by bit, concertinering it into the grip of one pincer, holding it firmly together. Once it had completed that feat, it began to tear off pieces of the worm and stuff them into its jaws.

We watched in horrified fascination, feeling deep pity for the unfortunate worm, hating the crab, but yet recognising that even crabs had to eat to live and that this was how they went about it.

I left before it had finished its meal, unable to bear the sight of the worm's agony. Soon afterwards, Peter found another huge specimen in the grass between the well and the stream, and then several more, smaller crabs. The discovery that they could be found in the long grass as well as the water, was a blow to my assumption that this was our little Eden, safe and without any sort of threat, (apart from the leeches!) as long as the cattle were grazing elsewhere. Having just watched one of the crabs feeding, I did not like the idea of sharing the meadow with such inhuman monsters, so I did not go back to the hollow tree for a while. Meanwhile, the V.A.s had left. The dinner party had been a farewell gathering in their honour. Life for us returned to its routine of walks and lessons. The paddling stream was at its best after the monsoon, before the oiling had to be resumed. We spent many mornings there, playing in the shallows and on the rocks while

Mother sat in the shade of a jak-fruit tree and sewed or wrote letters.

In the evenings, after our baths and our supper, we always spent a little while with Father, playing rough and tumble games with him, for at that time of day he would be relaxed and accessible as he sat beside the log fire that was lighted on most evenings during the cool season. Sometimes he would make up stories for us, based largely on his own adventures when he was a young man. The hero of the stories, he alleged, was a friend of his called Bill Smith. They took place in Africa where he had spent some years during and after the Second Boer War, trying and failing to make his fortune.

Bill Smith was carried down a river after inadvertently pitching his tent on top of a hippo, was rescued by an African tribe and fed on mealies, (maize meal) until his digestion gave out; then he somehow entered the world of termites in a termite mound!

All these tall tales were, of course, enchanting to us. Inevitably, alas, he began to run out of ideas, and became reluctant to yield to our demands for yet another 'Bill Smith' adventure.

One evening when we appeared in our dressing gowns for our time with him, he was engrossed in an article in the Overseas Magazine. He told us he was reading about breeding silver foxes, and showed us the pictures of them.

"But they're black, not silver!" I protested. I had expected to see shiny, metallic-looking animals.

" They have silver tips to their fur. The photo doesn't show that very well." He explained. "I'm going to buy two pairs of them."

He went on to explain that the people who were selling them, would look after them for him in England, and their cubs would be used for their fur, which, he said, was worth a lot of money. When we went home on leave, we would go and see them.

Neither Peter nor I could see how black foxes could deserve to be called silver, but it seemed that they, rather than the mine of real silver that we believed we had found, were going to make our fortunes.

CHRISTMAS

One of the best times of year was Christmas. The weather was still cool but fine. Sometimes on Christmas Day, our parents gave a party for their friends and their children. There would be tea and games for us, then one of the young bachelor planters would put on the Father Christmas costume that Mother kept hidden in a cupboard in her bedroom, and give out the presents. Unused as we were to the company of other children, we were shy and a bit resentful of the attention given to the visiting children. Most of them, with the exception of Betty and the Vansomeren boys, were strangers to us. This year, however, there was no party for us, though our parents were to go to one that evening.

The day began early. On the night before Christmas Eve, Mother had safety-pinned one of her stockings to the mosquito net at the head of each of our beds for Santa Claus to fill.

On Christmas morning I opened my eyes as it was beginning to grow light, probably woken by the crowing of the cockerel in the chicken run. I stretched out my hand to feel the stocking, hoping Santa had been. Yes, there it was, stiff and crackly. I pulled up the bottom of the net to undo the safety-pin. In his bed, Peter was doing likewise.

"He's been." he said.

"Yes," I said, "Happy Christmas!"

We struggled to unpack the contents; painting books whose corners caught in the fabric, though rolled into a cylinder to contain boxes of crayons, small tin paint boxes, little toys and a mouth-organ. In the toe, as always, there was an orange and some sweets. The shrill blasts of tin whistles and our excited voices awoke Mother, who came, wrapped in her kimono dressing gown, laughing at our delight in the contents of our stockings, and pretending to be amazed at Father Christmas's generosity.

"Look what he gave us!" we said, in all innocence, expecting her to be as eager as we were over to see what we had found.

There had been an occasion in the past, now legendary, when Robert succeeded in staying awake for Father Christmas. Next morning, to our awed amazement, he had related how he grabbed hold of the great man's robe to prevent him from escaping, but the mysterious visitor had managed to pull free and departed in haste from Robert's bedroom. For this daring deed, Robert achieving heroic status in the eyes of us children.

Every Christmas, Peter and I tried hard to keep awake to repeat Robert's escapade, but without success. In reality, I was well aware that I, for one, would never have been brave enough actually to seize hold of such a mysterious and legendary visitor.

After breakfast on Christmas morning, every year there took place a ritual in front of the bungalow. As we all

Christmas

stood together on the veranda, everybody who worked on the Estate, the teams of pluckers and their kanganis, the writers and clerks, the factory workers, the schoolmaster and his pupils would gather in the drive. The children sang one or two carols, somehow managing to transform them to sound like Tamil songs. They would also give a display of gymnastics that Mother referred to as 'Physical Jerks.' We would be garlanded with wreaths of yellow chrysanthemums, jasmine or marigolds that perfumed the air. Limes were pressed into our hands. The Rice Merchant would offer his lavish but unacceptable gifts, and more modest ones that were received with thanks. That year he brought us a wonderful clockwork circus, which, to our delight, we were allowed to accept.

After the workers had been paid their Christmas bonuses by the clerks, there followed a part of the annual ceremony devised by Mother. Trays of fudge were cut into squares and carried out by Francis and Kunichin, and passed along the rows of coolies, adults and children alike, for each one to help themselves. After that, and some sort of short address by Father, everyone would put their hands together and bow their thanks and file back towards the lines.

The ceremony over, we drove to church. The area in which we lived was too remote to support a full-time parson, but a preacher came to the church for the main religious feasts such as Christmas, Easter and Harvest Festival. I always found the services mystifying. I was unsure when to stand, sit or kneel, and the first time I was taken there, I thought the voice of the vicar intoning was the voice of God Himself, and was disappointed when I realised my mistake. After all, hadn't I been told we were in God's house?

The church was decorated with flowers and greenery from the gardens of the planters. The congregation was largely Indian, the local Tamil women in their best saris, brightening the grey stone church with their reds and blues, greens and oranges. The Malayalams wore spotless white as did most of the men. The European women wore their flowered dresses and topees or shady hats.

After the service, greetings were exchanged between the Europeans, then we drove home to a traditional English Christmas meal of roast Turkey and plum pudding. Mr Wilshaw, as a bachelor living alone, was invited to join us that Christmas. Sometimes he spent Christmas with the Gilbeys, his next nearest neighbours after us. Although Peter and I were shy of Mr Wilshaw, we liked and trusted him, unlike Father's other assistant, Mr Gowan, who we both disliked intensely. As luck would have it, Mr Gowan also made one of the party, for his wife had returned to Scotland to have their baby.

Mr Gowan seemed to delight in discomfiting us, and would tease us in ways we found difficult to respond to. My name gave him great scope for humour, and he never failed to ask me: "Where's Adam?" It taught me at an early age that bad jokes repeated frequently do not become witty.

As he sat holding the glass of whisky, habitual with him, Peter and I tried to see what it was that had persuaded a person as charming as his wife Mary to marry someone so hateful.

The sitting room and dining room had been decorated with sprigs of cedar and swags of scarlet plush above every picture. On the veranda a large cedar branch had been planted in a tub and hung with scarlet garlands and coloured glass baubles that looked like frozen soap bubbles, and fantastic birds with spun glass tails. Small barley-sugar-twist candles in brightly painted holders were clipped to the tips of the branches.

After our afternoon rest, they were lighted and burned with a brilliance diminished by the afternoon sunshine, in honour of the Christmases our parents remembered. Someone who bore a faint resemblance to Mr Wilshaw under the crimson robe and bushy white beard, gave out the presents. It was a somewhat subdued festival, but Peter and I preferred it to the false gaiety that attended the bigger gatherings of the neighbours.

It was sometime soon after that Christmas, (our last at Arnakal, though we did not know it,) that a puzzling incident took place. It so happened that Peter and I were playing in the garden near the dining room where our parents were talking together. The doors and windows were open wide, so that their voices carried out to us. We did not understand what was being said, but it seemed to us that they were arguing. What caught our attention and appalled us was that it was obvious that Mother was crying.

We rushed away to the lower garden, where we could no longer hear them, or be heard.

"I didn't think grown-ups could cry." said Peter.

"Neither did I." I said.

Crying, we knew was babyish. Children did it when they were hurt or someone was cross with them, but it was something that grown-ups never, ever did. Yet we had both observed it, Mother definitely seemed to be crying.

We did not discuss it further, but turned it over in our minds and brooded over it. What was important about it to us, was not the cause of her tears, (I thought it was probably something to do with a letter from Ann that had come that morning,) it was the fact that she was able to give way to what we were encouraged to think of as a weakness. Until then we had been of the opinion that grown-ups were unable to produce tears, and that it was something to do with how people changed as they matured.

We took care not to let her know that we had witnessed this moment of weakness, and she herself did not reveal to us that anything upsetting had happened. The cause remained a mystery.

Father, who we felt was most likely to have caused her tears, we regarded from then on, with more than our usual awe. We had learned something more about the strange world of adults, but at the same time we felt less at ease, our own world seemed less safe, for the very laws we had taken forgranted were now in question, since grown-ups were, after all, sometimes liable to shed tears.

THE LETTER

Sometime towards the end of January, Peter and I were busy under the rose-apple tree, planting seeds that Mother had given us for our garden, when we saw the tapil coolie come to the house with a bundle of letters, which he gave to Father who was in the garden with Mother. He shuffled through them and passed two or three letters from England to her, then he retired to his study with the rest, which seemed to be mostly uninteresting-looking long envelopes.

Presently, Father appeared on the veranda with a letter in his hand, and walked down the steps to where Mother was cutting the dead flowers off the roses. He showed the letter to her and they began to walk up and down the gravel drive, arm in arm, talking together with an air of great seriousness.

From where we were, busy digging among our plants, Peter and I realised that something important must have happened, but did not dare to interrupt our parents to ask what it was.

Later, during the afternoon walk, Mother asked: "What do you think about us all going Home?"

"What do you mean ?" I asked, "on leave? I thought we weren't going until next year."

"No, not leave. For good. We won't be coming back. Daddy's just heard that he's got the sack."

"What sack? Why does he want a sack? Are we never coming back?" We were dismayed at the thought." When are we going?"

"Not for a little while yet." Mother explained. "The sack means that Daddy has lost his job. When the V.A.s were here they decided that Daddy wasn't well enough to manage the Estate. The Market is bad at the moment so they can't get the right price for our tea. It's so stupid, really, because he's been so much fitter since his operation."

"What will we do? What about the bungalow and all our things?" We had endless questions to ask, and Mother answered as best she could.

"We'll find something, don't worry. We don't have to leave for a little while yet. Probably Mr Gowan will take over, as he's the senior S.D."

Later we were told that it had been Mr Gowan who had persuaded Mr Sylvester and Mr Barker that a man of our father's age, (he was in his fifties,) and state of health was not robust enough to manage an estate the size of Arnakal. In truth Mr Gowan was a man consumed by ambition and now he had a wife and child to support, he coveted the Manager's salary and the larger bungalow. The V.A.s had no idea, for it was not revealed by Father, that already there had been the three attempts on his life, he was so hated by the coolies. Nowadays he always carried his lead-weighted walking stick with him as a means of defence.

The Letter

Little account was taken of the fact that, during the fourteen years he had been Manager of the estate, Father had opened up nearly a thousand acres of jungle, improved the roads through the estate and almost eliminated malaria from the district.

For a little while our lives continued much as usual but at the same time, everything seemed to be changing.

One afternoon, we were walking towards the dam with Mother when the dogs who, as usual, had run ahead of us, stopped in their tracks and began to bark furiously at something on the path. The hair along their backs was bristling and they were dancing, stiff-legged in a semicircle, showing a mixture of aggression and fear before whatever it was that disturbed them.

As we caught up with them, we saw that lying across the path like a bright green ribbon, was a snake. It had reared up, its upper body erect, its head swaying this way and that towards the dogs, while from its scaly lipless mouth its forked tongue flickered. We all stood still and stared at it.

Creatures of my nightmares as snakes were, I had scarcely ever seen a live one. We were always warned to be careful while walking in long undergrowth in case we trod on one. Perhaps it was these warnings, or was it a primal instinct? Whatever the reason, I had a terror of snakes. I did not mind so much the cobras brought by the snake charmers that sometimes came to perform to us. I was assured that these had had their fangs removed. But still, had I been asked, I would not have been able to touch them.

Mother and Peter caught the dogs, fastened their leads and pulled them away to try to calm them. None of us knew what to do next, and stood watching the creature, so terrifying, yet so beautiful with its pale belly and shining emerald scales.

Just then a coolie came up behind us, striding barefoot along the road. When he saw what we were staring at, he muttered something in Tamil, which we did not understand, then picked up a thick stick from beside the path. He moved so swiftly and so surely that I scarcely saw the blow as he struck the snake just below its head, breaking its back. He beat the writhing body once or twice, then, lifting it with the end of the stick he tossed it, still twitching, into the bushes beside the track and, smiling at our thanks, continued on his way.

The snake caught on a branch and hung limply there, white belly uppermost like a green and white cord. A moment before it had been so beautiful for all its menace and implied evil, but now it hung, a sad sordid thing, blood dripping from its wounds, its jewel-bright eyes growing dull.

On our way back, we noted that it had already begun to shrivel in the sun, the blood turning black as it dried. Flies had gathered and were swarming round it, buzzing greedily.

The incident made a deep impression on us all and for me it added to my growing sense of unease. Our little world, where we had lived in the confidence and perfect trust that no evil existed there, suddenly seemed to be threatening us.

Soon after this incident, I caught sight of a long brown snake sliding across my path and into the tea bushes that bordered the garden near the Estate Office. It vanished from sight in seconds, but for a moment I found myself

The Letter

standing frozen with fright, unable to move until I was sure it was no longer to be seen.

Some days later I decided to go back to visit the hollow tree. I thought I would cut the grass that had grown long round the roots, so took a pair of shears with me.

My first action was to make for the stream to see if the crabs were still there. The water level had dropped, and to my relief, there was no sign of the creatures, just the water flowing crystal clear over the pebbles and sand. Reassured, I went back to the tree and began to snip the grass.

It was then that I heard it, a sudden rustle in the dead leaves that lay among the roots where I stood.

I froze, and listened for a second before glancing down towards my feet just in time to see that what I had taken to be one of the roots on the surface of the ground, was moving.

Terrified, I glimpsed what I took to be a hooded head disappearing into the shadows of the bushes, followed by the long grey-brown body of a snake. To my horror I realised that in another second I might have trodden on it, or, worse still, snipped it with the shears.

The idea was too horrifying to think about, so I turned and fled back to the bungalow, where, gasping for breath, I told Peter what I had just seen.

When Father heard my tale, he took his shotgun and went down to see if the snake was still there, but found nothing. However, as a precaution, he told us to keep away from the tree from then on. It was an order we found easy to obey.

If it really was a cobra, it could be very dangerous for us. When alarmed cobras sometimes spit their venom at their attacker, with results as fatal as a bite.

After that I began to feel that everything was changing for the worse. First, the crabs had invaded the meadow, and now snakes were nesting in the tree, making it another place that had become taboo to me. I still did not want to go alone to the area close to the bottlebrush tree in the lower garden where I had tried so unsuccessfully to bury the kittens. I was haunted by the memory of those little bloated exhumed bodies laid out on the grass.

By now the bungalow seemed to be cluttered with packing cases and tea chests. The trunks were brought out of the box room, dusted free of cobwebs and left open in the sun to remove the smell of mildew that was endemic to the humidity of the climate. The cedar chest that always stood in the long passage was filled with linen and curtains and placed in a crate that the local carpenter had made for that purpose. Books, pictures, china, glass and pots and pans were wrapped in newspaper and packed in wood-shavings, ready to be collected and taken to be put aboard a cargo ship and transported to England.

Homes had to be found for the dogs. Mr Gowan would not want them, he disliked animals.

Mickey was offered a home some hundred miles away towards Mundakayam. Kunichin took him there by bus.

Independent and unfriendly towards us, as Mickey had always been, nonetheless we missed him. He had always refused to allow us to pat or stroke him and snapped at us if we tried to do so, but at the same time, he always seemed pleased to see us and willingly came for walks with us.

Digger was to go to live with a near neighbour. He was far more amenable and willing to be made a fuss

The Letter

of, added to which he was a good watchdog with his propensity to bark at strangers. He was to stay with us until nearer our departure date.

A week or so after Mickey had gone, the tapil coolie cycled up to the house with a letter to Mother from Mickey's new owners. She read it and began to laugh. Then she read it out to Peter and me:

"He bit us when we stroked him," The letter ran, "Then he made a mess in the house, and when I smacked him, he bit me again. He got into a fight with the pariah dogs in the Lines and was lame in one foot, but would not let us treat it. Soon afterwards he disappeared and has not been seen for a week."

That very afternoon, looking thin and a bit bedraggled, and limping on three legs, Mickey turned up in the garden. He was obviously delighted to have found us again, wagging his stumpy tail in happiness. It was hard to believe that he had found his way so far, along an unknown route, but there he was and there was no other way to explain that fact.

After he had been fed, we managed to hold him between us, with a towel round his head so he could not get his teeth into us while we bathed and bandaged his foot.

Soon after we had finished, he tore the bandage off again, but in a few days it began to heal.

Mother found someone else, this time a neighbour who was willing to take him.

"He's a man's dog," she said, as he was taken off to the bachelor planter's home.

But he did not stay there long. Arnakal was his home, but he was not owned by anyone. He was a small black partly-spaniel dog with an outsized spirit of independence. In the end, we were later informed, he went off to live wild with the village pye (pariah) dogs.

The day came when a lorry took all the packing cases and most of the trunks (save for those needed on our voyage home) The bungalow had a stark, unfamiliar atmosphere. Days passed with the sense of our approaching departure heavy in the air.

On one hand, as our parents tried to emphasise, we were going to see Robert and Ann again, and the aunts and uncles whom we knew only from letters at Christmas and birthdays. We were going Home.

On the other hand, Home was an unknown place, remembered dimly from our six month stay three years ago, when Peter had been only three and I five years old.

Was I never to see again this place where I was born? Never more see the surrounding hills that shaded from green to violet into the distance? Never more bathe in the cool flowing stream or play innocently naked on its rocky shore in the morning sun? Never more be grumbled at by Francis or Kunichin, or hear the evening bugle echoing over the hills?

Down by the tennis court the mahogany tree which every year dropped one branch and grew taller, would annually continue to shed its branches and grow without us, until one day a storm would blow it down. We were never to know, as Peter and I had often speculated, whether it would be tall enough to reach to the house when it fell. The orange trees and the pawpaws would fruit for Mr and Mrs Gowan. His child would swing on our swing in the lower garden, amongst the azaleas and the pink bottlebrush mimosa.

The Letter

We were roused from sleep one night, and taken in our pyjamas to the front of the house where the hired car was waiting, our own car having been bought by the local taxi driver. The luggage rack at the rear was being piled high with trunks and suitcases. Wrapped in blankets, we stood in the drive. The moon was just rising, and the servants were holding a hurricane lantern as they stood in a group to bid us 'farewell'.

During the weeks before this night the neighbours had held parties and a dance at the Club to wish our parents 'God Speed' and to say 'Goodbye'. The day before, a Farewell Ceremony had taken place with all the Estate staff mustering in front of the bungalow, very much as at Christmas. Speeches were made honouring Father for all the years he had worked there. We were garlanded with gold and silk garlands, and many wreaths of chrysanthemums and roses. Limes were pressed into our hands, and a presentation was made to our father of a cylindrical stand made of ebony, held by a pair of stylised ebony elephants, to symbolise the name 'Arnakal' or ' Elephant Rock'. It contained scrolls made of silk and printed with copies of the speeches in gold letters.

Now, as the moon rose and added its cold light to that of the lantern, Francis, Kunichin and Muthu, and even the sweeper woman and her son, and Totemcurran were there to see us go. Kunichin was sniffing, and I saw him wipe his eyes with the back of his hand as he wished us 'Good Luck'. Our parents repeated their last instructions as to what needed to be done in the morning after we had gone, and wished them well with their new employers. All had been found new posts. None of them was willing to work for Mr Gowan.

We got into the car. Peter and I sat in the back with Mother, wrapped in blankets and surrounded by cushions and packages.

I stared through the window as we drove away up the shadow-striped avenue to the factory. In the moonlight, the factory, the jak tree, and the bullock carts beneath it were as insubstantial as dreams.

The car's engine laboured under its heavy load. Pye dogs ran yapping after us as we drove through the lines. Silently, I was saying: "Goodbye. Goodbye. One day I promise to come back." I was too proud to let my tears be seen, so I let them slip down my cheeks in silence, and turned my head to wipe them away on the cushions. My feelings were beyond words. It was as if we were being expelled from Paradise, leaving the serpent in possession. Added to the pain of leaving, was the thought that of all people, it was to be Mr Gowan who would live in our bungalow.

Mother said to Peter: "Eve's very quiet. She must be asleep."

Far from sleeping, I was trying to memorise every inch of the journey.

We skirted Vandiperyar. Everyone was asleep, even the pigs were slumbering beside the road. As we entered the jungle at the top of the ghat there was sudden crash from behind us. The car pulled up, the driver and Father got out and walked round to see what had happened.

The luggage rack had broken and the trunks and cases lay strewn across the road behind us. There was a delay as, by the dim light of the moon and a torch, they untied the ropes that had held it all together, and lashed the broken luggage rack back once more before fastening the cases on

The Letter

again. There was a sense of urgency as they worked, for we had to reach the station, sixty miles of winding road away, in time to catch the train.

Finally the load was back in place, more securely tied this time, and we began the long descent down the ghat. Dawn was breaking, and the trees emerged dimly through the morning mist. Birds began to call. There was the familiar cry of the junglefowl, clear and sweet; pigeons, bulbuls and the harsh croak of crows. Some of the trees were hung with cobwebs that sparkled in the growing light with dewdrop diamonds. A waterfall fell in a long column like the tail of a gigantic horse, and roared beneath the road with the voice of dragons.

The road zigzagged down the hillsides as the sun rose behind us, until, at last we reached the station. It was Easter morning, the first of April, a bright sunny day.

Sleepy and dazed from the long journey, we washed and dressed in the waiting room with a growing sense of excitement. For the moment we forgot our sadness, as we sat down to breakfast of coloured eggs that had been arranged for us, and waited for the train.

There in the unfamiliar surroundings of the railway station, watching the monkeys playing in the trees across the line, with the prospect of several days rail journey ahead of us, we began to feel a sense of adventure. Our parents were relaxed and cheerful, speaking about the things we would see on our way. They were postponing anxious thoughts of the uncertainties of starting a new life, of finding a way to support four children and adapt to life in England at a time of economic depression, and after a lifetime in the East.

On that Easter Day, breakfasting in the cool of the early morning, while we waited for the train, we saw the future as an adventure, a new beginning.

THE VOYAGE HOME

After the long journey by train, we reached Columbo, and spent a few days with Mother's sister and her husband on their rubber plantation in Ceylon, where Mother had met and married Father fourteen years before. Afterwards, in Columbo, we boarded the ship that was to carry us away , finally and forever, from India and our beloved Arnakal.

The ship proved to be a consolation for all we were losing and Peter and I were very happy on board. It was not our first sea voyage. Four years earlier we had travelled to England when Father had taken his last leave. We had returned to India a year later, but because we had been much younger, we were consequently more restricted in what we were allowed to do. In addition, the Banranald was a greatly superior vessel to either the Baradine or the Barabul, the liners we had previously sailed on. A recent addition to the P&O fleet of liners, it was one of the first to be powered by oil instead of coal, and therefore was much cleaner. Other advantages, from a child's viewpoint, included a purpose built swimming pool with steps down into shallow and deep ends instead of a steep-sided canvas tank into which children had to be lowered by their parents.

In spite of our two previous sea journeys, we had to relearn all the correct nautical terms such as companionway for stairs, deck for floor, portholes for windows and so on. It took a few days before we acquired our sea-legs and stopped feeling nauseated by the movements of the ship. Having acquired them, we enjoyed running along the gangway between the cabins, while never being quite sure at each step when our feet would connect with the deck.

There were a dozen or so other children, of mixed ages, on board. Entertainments were arranged for us, parties and games, but much of the time we amused each other or we roamed about, exploring the ship.

The Grown-ups sat about in the Saloon lounge or reclined on deck in long canvas chairs. The swimming pool opened in the morning and in the late afternoon when the sun was not too fierce, and there was a court marked out on one of the decks for quoits, played with a circle of rope. Some of the men tried to play football, but very soon into the game the ball was lost overboard.

All around us the sea sparkled and we never tired of watching the waves that curled and foamed each side of the ship as it cut through the water. We looked out for flying fish and porpoises. Gulls followed us and rested on the tops of the masts and the funnels.

It was a time without stress, an interlude between being uprooted and torn away from the life we had known from our birth and replanted in the strange new country known as 'Home', with the prospect ahead of school, all of which was unimaginable. All the knowledge I had of boarding school was culled from the 1928 edition of The Boy's Own Annual, which had belonged to my elder brother, Robert. It had conveyed the view that girls were an altogether inferior species, given easily to tears, reluctant to climb trees or do anything strenuous, and prone to tale-telling, therefore not to be trusted. It also made clear that decent people i.e. boys, always stuck up for their friends, never told lies or informed on anyone, and were brilliant at games such as cricket or rugger, which, of course no girl could play. This view was to cause me a lot of trouble when I went to school, but that was still in the future.

I made friends with a boy of my own age called Mark. He was a good looking child with fair hair and an equable temperament, who seemed to have the gift of thinking up new games to play whenever we began to get bored: forms of tag or hide and seek, or simply make believe. In the little group that chose to play with us, he and I, aged nine, were the eldest, and the leaders.

There was another small group, a family of four or five boys, young teenagers, who we regarded with distrust. They jeered at our innocent childish games and disrupted them with rough wildness, showing off and boasting about how tough they were, mavericks, always up to mischief, always in trouble. The mothers of the younger children led their charges away when the Brady boys came on the scene.

The rest of us were a goody-goody bunch, disinclined to stray far from our parents wishes, but the Bradys were constantly called to order by their perpetually furious father and mother. In spite of this, before we reached England, the boys were to prove to be capable of a

The Tea Planter's Children

recklessness none of us could have imagined to be possible in a child.

There was a break in the voyage when the Banranald stopped at Adan for refuelling. The passengers were allowed ashore and our parents took Peter and me on a coach tour of the surrounding country. It was unbearably hot in the bus as we drove through a landscape of barren volcanic rock, grey, treeless and arid. We were taken to see the Roman wells, and then to an oasis where a grove of palm trees cast feathery shadows over a pool, and there were birds singing among their fronds.

Peter and I longed for ices. Instead we were given glasses of warm lemonade before we climbed into the bus again to return to the ship. We were not sorry to leave Aden aboard the Banranald, where the air in the saloon was cooled by fans and there were ices for dessert.

As we travelled through the Red Sea we performed a ceremony Mother had taught us on our last voyage. She took us to the rear of the ship where we threw overboard our topees, the cork sun hats we needed to wear in the tropics, We watched as they were left behind, tumbling over and over in the wake until they were out of sight. We speculated over the strangers who might find them washed up on some sandy shore.

Suez was next. We passed slowly through the canal, the ship's engine was shut down as it was drawn through the locks. Arabs walked along either bank holding ropes to prevent the ship swinging into the banks. The journey took most of the day. We stood along the rails with the other passengers to watch as in the distance camel trains stalked through the dunes. However, we soon grew tired of watching and went away to play.

The Voyage Home

As we travelled through the Mediterranean Mother speculated whether we would see Mount Etna, but we passed it during the night while we slept. After Malta the weather became noticeably cooler, and the passengers were allowed to visit the luggage hold to unpack their warm clothes.

Until then we children liked playing on the top deck, where there was always a cooling breeze. Now the breezes grew stronger and the grown ups preferred more sheltered places to sit so we were left a good deal to our own devices. The hatches made level platforms where we liked to play, but when the weather turned windy, the tarpaulin cover would fill with air and billow upwards. A favourite game was to jump on the billows and squash out the air but Mark and I agreed that what we really wanted was to be carried up as the cover rose, only we were too heavy and the tarpaulin always refused to rise for us.

By now we were entering the Bay of Biscay. "The Bay Of Biscuits" we repeated endlessly, relishing the joke each time it was repeated. We had been warned by our parents that the sea was likely to be very rough through the Bay, and we soon realised the truth of that. Peter and Mother succumbed to seasickness, as did many of the passengers. Mark and I, unaffected, were left more than ever to amuse ourselves with the few remaining children who were not seasick.

Then on one particular day, we had congregated as usual on the top deck. Peter had got over his sickness and joined us, together with half a dozen other hardy youngsters, and one or two adults keeping a desultory eye on us. The wind blew, the hatch cover rose and we tried again and again to be carried up on it, without success.

Mark and I tried to persuade the younger children to try. They all were afraid of being blown away, except for one little boy, David, a favourite with us all because he was so friendly and trusting, always willing to be a baby or a dog as required by the game in progress. His mother, who had a small baby as well, seeing that we seemed fond of him and that we appeared to be sensible children, sometimes left him in our charge. This was so that day.

The ship was rolling heavily, the waves crashed down as it ploughed through them, flinging spray across the decks which was very exciting. Sometimes the ship rolled until the waves came above the portholes.

Mark, Peter and I had tried with our usual lack of success to ride the hatchcover balloon, when we decided that, as a treat, we would let David have a turn. We placed the three year old in the middle of the hatch and stood back to await the next gust. Suddenly, up sailed David, perched on the top of the billow. We shrieked with delight. David was shrieking too. It took a minute or two before we realised that his cries were not of delight but terror as he tried to cling to the smooth extended canvas, with the sea raging below him and the ship leaning as if to tip him into the waves. Mark and I leapt up to trample the bubble flat and reached him as the ship righted itself. We lifted him off. He was sobbing and furious with us, no longer the sweet amiable child we knew. Just as we lifted him off, who should arrive on the scene but the Brady boys.

"What's going on?" they asked. They saw David angrily push us away as we tried to comfort him.

"What's wrong with the kid?" asked Tom Brady, the eldest of the gang.

Reluctantly we gave a brief summary of the cause for David's tears.

"Oh, David! you poor kid. Don't have anything to do with them, come and play with us."

Despite our protests, David staggered down the sloping deck and ran across to them. The boys took his hands and bent down to him.

"Would you like us to give you a swing?" they said.

David, beginning to smile through his tears, nodded. Holding his hands and feet, they began to swing him back and forth. The ship had righted itself and was beginning to roll the other way.

"Like to look at the waves, Davy?" asked Barry, the next oldest. He was a sharp faced, skinny boy of about twelve.

We three stood resentfully watching them as they lifted the little boy up and then froze in horror at what came next. Still holding his hands and ankles, they hoisted him level with the top the rail, and then leaned out until he was suspended over the side of the ship, above the seething, swirling water.

Shrieking, we rushed towards them. As the ship began to level out again, they lifted him back. We seized David and dragged him away.

"What's up with you?" said Tom as the other boys laughed." He loved it, didn't you, Davy?"

"We'll tell the Captain!" shouted Peter as we led the little boy away. He was sobbing again.

"Yar! We didn't do any thing, did we. Sissies!" the boys jeered.

"Come on, we'll give you a go to show you." said Tom, grabbing Peter, but Peter, twice David's age, put up a fierce struggle to get free. Mark and I went to help him, but luckily at that moment some of the crew came on to the deck to check the lifeboats, and ordered us all below, saying that it wasn't safe for us to be there unsupervised.

David's mother also appeared to take him for his lunch. Most of the other children had been behind the hatch out of the wind, and had seen nothing of what had happened.

When we got back to the cabin in, we reported the incident to our father.

"Is this true?" he asked, looking shocked, "If it is true, I must tell the Captain. You say that they actually held the child over the rail? You're quite sure of that?"

"Yes," I said.

"Yes, it's true." said Peter, "right over the sea. They wanted to do it to me too, but I got away."

There were questions asked. The Captain sent for the boys and their parents, but they denied everything. David was thought to be too young to be a reliable witness, but the boys' parents were ordered to keep them under strict supervision for the rest of the voyage. This made their father more bad tempered than ever, but they were shut up in their cabin from then on and we only saw them at meal times.

The rest of us were forbidden to use the top deck without our parents.

It was cold, with a thin drizzle as we sailed up the Channel. Seagulls flocked overhead, the cliffs of Dover loomed white and green through the mist. A pilot boarded to take the ship into Tilbury. As we reached the place our parents called Home, the adventures of the voyage was already receding into a dream. Mark, David and the

Bradys went their separate ways to live their lives, and we, reunited with our older brother and sister, began the rest of ours.

GOING BACK

Our departure from India in the April of 1934 was the end of an idyll. Soon after reaching England, Peter and I were sent away to boarding schools, and Father, whose health was never robust, had been unable to adapt to England and its climate after a lifetime in the East and died three years later. All that is another story.

After the isolation of Arnakal, the girl's boarding school came as a great shock, and even though I was with my sister Ann, who had been a pupil there for the three years we were in India, I found it difficult to fit in. My childhood experiences had been quite different from those of my companions and I was unused to being with large numbers of children. I was very homesick, escaping into the world of books, and dreams of the blue familiar hills and the well remembered paths of Arnakal. I would imagine that I was wandering through the bungalow and relive the things that Peter and I had done together, promising myself that one day I would go back. Throughout my life it remained a kind of Shangri-La, a place of eternal peace and happiness.

Going Back

When my own children began to leave home I started to write down my Indian memories as short stories for the Writers' Group I had joined and later hosted, but it took sixty-four years to realise my dream of returning there. Then in October 1998, it at last became possible for me to travel back to India to stay once more in the bungalow at Arnakal.

This came about through my daughter Sarah, who five years earlier, while travelling in South India with a friend, had decided to visit the place where I had been born. David K. had only recently been installed as Manager, but he and his wife, Mona made Sarah welcome and allowed her to photograph whatever she liked. In these, when she showed them to me, the bungalow looked very much as I remembered it.

I sent copies of Sarah's pictures to the K.s, together with some taken by my mother from similar view-points, and so began a correspondence with Mona. I was, by that time, thinking of making my stories into a book and she was able to help me with my researches. She also invited me to stay with them if ever I went back.

On hearing that I intended going back to see Arnakal again, Peter said he would like to come with me. My husband had reservations about travelling to India, and since this was to be a journey of reminiscences that he would be unable to share, he chose not to accompany us.

Since one of the purposes of going back was to verify the background to my memoir, having Peter with me, with his own recollections to compare with mine, could only be helpful.

So it was that we found ourselves in Trivandrum, with the feeling of familiarity combined with strangeness that was to be our experience throughout our visit. The passage of sixty years and independence from British rule had, naturally enough, brought many changes; more cars and buses; telephones; electric fans; air-conditioning; satellite dishes, where we had known only bullock carts; man-drawn rickshaws; paraffin lamps, and punkas. India changes slowly, and there was much that remained the same, but now we saw it from the perspective of a life spent in Britain. The traffic in the city was horrendous, with shoals of auto-rickshaws, (bright yellow, two-seater cabs powered by a motorbike engine) putt-putting in and out of the stream of vehicles, everyone driving with their thumbs firmly on their hooters, and set on overtaking anything ahead.

The beggars had not changed. They sat at the roadside; men with terrible deformities, caused by polio or leprosy; women with tiny, half-naked babies asleep on the ground beside them and young children with one hand outstretched, the other miming putting food into their mouths; people apparently in the last stages of starvation, who wrung our heart-strings.

Churches of all denominations and mosques rub shoulders with Hindu temples and shrines, bright with painted statues of dancing gods and animals; many imposing buildings behind high walls, shaded by big trees. The Institute of Homeopathy, the College of Ayurovedic Medicine, University College to name a few, not forgetting the Residency, a long white building with classical porticoes, now the seat of Government.

Going Back

Peter and I had decided to spend a day or two in Travandrum to adjust to the change in time and climate, and also because we both were tentative about actually seeing Arnakal again since it was emotionally of such huge importance. I discovered that Peter's feelings about this return to the place for which we had so many cherished memories, was as ambivalent as mine. Would we regret it? Would it be harder afterwards to recall those images that had given us comfort throughout our lives?

I telephoned Arnakal on our first evening. It was the first time I had spoken to the K.s, and was reassured by David's voice, slow with the sound of a smile through the Indian lilt, and Mona's, welcoming but at the same time a little shy. I said we would like to go there on the Thursday, three days hence.

In the mean while, we retraced our steps to the zoo and were surprised how different it was. Where I remembered it as being open and lacking in shade, there was now a wooded park with lakes and huge over-shadowing trees, among which were scattered the cages and paddocks. The park was beautiful though some of the paddocks were small and grazed bare and the cages had protective wire-netting over the bars. Notices in Tamil, Malayalam and English warned visitors against shouting or throwing things at the animals!

The next day we hired a taxi to take us to the coast at Kovalum. On the journey there we passed many small villages amongst coconut groves, where women sat at the roadside breaking stones with hammers; paddy fields and backwaters where, like drifts of snow, flocks of egrets fished among the beds of water hyacinths and lotuses.

Our memories of which beaches we had been to, were dim, and neither of us was sure whether, as children, we had stayed at Kovalum, or Cape Comoryn. However, we both recalled being shown over a lighthouse. Now authorisation is required before anyone is allowed within the fence that surrounds the one at Kovalum.

We walked along the palm-fringed shore accompanied by a gang of juvenile vendors, competing with each other to sell us bead necklaces and beach mats, desperate because, they insisted, there had been few tourists, though we could see several other Europeans basking on the sand.

When we had shaken off the children, we found a restaurant with the inviting name of "Paradise Cafe", an open-fronted shack with a few shabby tables and chairs. We asked for fresh coconut milk, and watched as a young man climbed a nearby palm tree to gather the nuts for us.

We ate a simple but delicious curry there, then made our way back through the renewed pleadings of the little vendors, ("You will come back? Promise. Promise. You really promise, don't you? My name is Ranji,(or Munju.) Don't buy from any one else, only from me, promise!") to where our taxi driver was waiting.

On Wednesday morning, we went to Trivandrum station, where, amid the queues and bustle, we unravelled the mysteries of booking a seat on the express train to Kottayam. An obliging porter helped us to fill in the necessary form, and when we turned up in the afternoon with our luggage, there he was with a companion, waiting to take our cases. Piling them on their heads, they strode off through the crowds, while we followed as best we could. The train was standing in the station, so our porters checked our seats and lodged our cases in the overhead rack.

Although time tabled as an Express, the train rolled along in an unhurried way, stopping at every station, and sometimes seemingly where no station was. It averaged less than thirty miles an hour. The slowness of this journey left me with a puzzle. When as children, we had taken the train, as I believed from Kottayam to Trivandrum, we had had berths and travelled through the night. It was of course, the days of steam locomotives, and there had been a long stop-over in wayside station while we dined in the restaurant car and perhaps there were other stops for refuelling, the fuel probably being wood. However, our journey that Wednesday was slow at three hours. I found it difficult to understand the time-difference. I remembered clearly that we left Kottayam at about seven in the evening, and reached Trivandrum after stopping somewhere for breakfast. A difference of ten hours was impossible to understand.

(Sometime after the end of this journey, I came across a letter written by Mother on headed paper from Arnakal, which included in the address the words: Kodai Karnal Station. This accounts for the discrepancies in my memory of the length of the train journey, and the appearance of the station, then small and plagued by hordes of monkeys. Perhaps the station at Kottayam, (now a busy junction without a monkey in sight!) was not yet built in the Thirties. However, at the time I believed we were retracing the route we had travelled on that last journey.)

Because both David and Mona would be unable to be home before the late afternoon, we passed the following morning very pleasantly aboard a boat on nearby Lake Venabad.

After lunch, we climbed into the elderly Ambassador, which by now we had come to realise was the vehicle universally favoured by Indian taxi drivers, and began the long journey up the ghat, crossing the years that had passed since we had come down this road, as I believed, to the railway at Kottayam, on the first stage of our voyage to the place our parents called 'Home.' I had stared out of the window of the car, trying to memorise every inch of the way, but sadly, had inevitably forgotten much. Besides, so much had changed.

We climbed the ghat in the midst of a stream of buses; cars and motorcycles that filled the air with the sound of their horns, and drove past the villages that crowded along the edges of the road. There had been coconut and plantain groves on that last journey, but neither of us recalled seeing rubber plantations at that altitude.

It was only a week or two since the end of what had been a long and exceptionally wet monsoon, so the landscape was lush and green, but where I remembered jungle, the hillsides were for the most part cultivated, with only small patches of wilderness left.

After driving for an hour or so, we reached the waterfall we both remembered, "falling in a long white column like the tail of a giant horse, roaring under the road with the voice of dragons." Below the road, it was now harnessed to a hydroelectric generator. We paused to take photographs beside parked lorries and a stall selling Coca-Cola.

During our ascent, we met herds of cattle and buffaloes being driven to market, the animals linked in pairs by tying their horns together. We overtook sad-looking elephants, huge and dusty, bearing logs that were tied to their flanks with ropes, moving slowly along the edge of the road behind their mahouts.

Peter reminded me of the time when we were coming up the ghat, and Mother, trying to avoid an approaching lorry, let the car slip into a monsoon drain. A long queue of bullock-carts and lorries had formed in both directions, before it was lifted back on to the road again.

The ghat was still narrow, but the surface was tarred and reasonably smooth, the valley side protected by a low wall. We began to notice trees with scarlet flowers, flame-of-the-forest, or flamboyants, whose existence I had forgotten, and the roadsides, especially near the villages, were brilliant with blue convolvulus, roses, bougainvillaea, hibiscus and, everywhere, the pink and orange-flowered lantana. As we reached the upper slopes at about three thousand feet, the trees began to give way to the low shrubs of the tea plantations.

"I'm sure they used not to grow like that." said Peter. I agreed. Where we remembered terraced rows of separate bushes, they seemed to be growing closer together, running into each other with wide, flat tops, like privet hedges.

At this higher altitude the air was noticeably cooler, and misty from low clouds. As the afternoon wore on, we came on a scene previously unknown to us, as neatly uniformed children were leaving the schools and convents to walk home, or wait for the school bus.

The plantations had provided schools, usually in a hut where the children sat cross-legged on the floor and wrote on slates; providing a very basic attempt at education with a single schoolmaster employed to teach all ages up to about twelve. (Of course, in the remoter parts of Britain at that time, many village schools were little better equipped). Now here were all these smiling, well dressed young people in chattering groups, carrying their satchels and briefcases on their way home, a demonstration of Kerala's claim to over 90% literacy.

We reached Vandiperiyar, and our memories became sharper. While the driver got out to ask the way to Arnakal, we looked around us and saw that the bridge across the Periyar now had railings on each side, not the stone parapet along which four-year old brother Robert, to the horror of the groom who had taken him out for a ride, had insisted on balancing. The rock-strewn riverbed lies some twenty feet below!

At the town end of the bridge there had once been a store where Mother bought gumboots and sandals for us, and sometimes boiled sweets. It was here that Robert, after balancing his way across the bridge, compounded his crime by purchasing two Christmas stockings, a large one for himself and a small one for Ann, charging them to Mother's account. The shop was gone without trace, and now across the road on the end of the bridge there was a tiny stone building, no bigger than a cupboard, boasting in scarlet letters, "Electrical Engineers. T.V. and Radios."

The town had grown from the remembered street with a bazaar, though there were still little booths along the sides of the road, selling saris, fruit, fish, pots, pans and so on. Where once, the bullock carts had to weave their way through the market as best they could amongst the chickens and goats and other livestock on sale, now politicians broadcast their speeches through loudspeakers, and cars and taxis clogged the street. The black pigs, closely resembling wild boar, no longer scavenge in the open drains, long gone together with the pariah dogs.

Having been told the way to Arnakal by several people, the taxi driver drove back across the bridge and turned on to a narrow road beside an electricity substation, (another sign of the way life had improved in the intervening years.) The road was little more than a track through the tea plantations. It was clear that there had once been a tarred surface, for here and there were remnants of tar, but most of it had been eroded by monsoon rain and traffic, leaving pot holes and boulders that even at the snail's pace we were travelling, shook and jarred us every inch of the way.

The driver looked understandably depressed for he was going to have to come back over that riverbed of a road again. We were beginning to wonder if it were really possible for this to be the right road, when, to our surprise, a vehicle came bouncing down towards us, "Arnakal Estate Ambulance" painted over the cab, and as we squeezed past, the driver confirmed that this was indeed the way to the estate. Our entry to Arnakal Estate itself was marked by a sudden improvement in the road surface, so that the driver was able to increase his speed to above the walking pace he'd been forced to maintain. Eagerly we began looking for familiar landmarks. There was the huge boulder sticking out of the hill, which we had always thought ought to be the elephant rock after which Arnakal had been named. (Later we were to learn that there is another rocky outcrop that claims that title.) The clump of scrub that grew in a fissure on its back, resembling, we used to think, a howdah, had grown into

The Tea Planter's Children

a large tree with spreading boughs. The eta grass that had covered the lower hillside, where I used to suspect tigers lurked, had been replaced by tea. Across the road, the grassy hill where, walking in a shower of rain, Peter and I had been sure we saw the end of a rainbow, was now uniformly clothed in the dark green bushes.

In the valley below us, we could see a rushing, rocky stream that we recognised as the one in which we used to paddle.

Groups of men and women were leaving the plantation, the women carrying strips of hessian, knotted to form sacks to hold the tea they had picked, instead of the baskets we had known.

Some large steel and concrete modern buildings came into view. We realised this must be the new factory, huge compared with the factory we remembered. Later we discovered that one of the buildings was the cardamom-drying warehouse, part of the spice industry that now augmented the tea. A pile of logs was neatly stacked behind the steel gates of the factory. "So," I thought, "they still fuel the furnaces with wood," and was pleased at the familiar sight, which told me that we were very close to our destination.

Now that we knew we were close to the house, our feelings were more than ever a mixture of excitement and apprehension as to what we would find on reaching this place where we spent so much of our childhood, and anxiety as to how the family, whose home it now was, felt about our return. We looked for the avenue that led down towards the house and there it was.

I wrote in the opening chapter of "The Tea Planter's Children": "The bungalow was situated a little below the crest of a small hill surrounded by other hills....It sprawled at the end of an avenue of feathery acacia trees." Now the avenue was spectacular with huge flame-of-the-forest trees, their fallen blossoms making a scarlet carpet before us.

"First there were the big green wooden gates on which Peter and I used to swing." The gates were gone, in their place a cattle grid and metal gates folded back. "Then came the garage with its tall faded green doors." The garage had vanished, leaving no trace, so too, the rose-apple trees we used to climb, which had overhung my garden where once grew the lilies that never flowered. The tall tree growing there may have been the one that was home to a cicada that Peter and I located, elusive insects though they are. A flourishing deliciosa vine now clothed its trunk, and little stripy squirrels, unfamiliar to us when we lived there, were playing in its branches.

"Opposite the house was a tennis court made of red latterite, and overlooking the court, but rooted beyond the wire netting fence, grew a mahogany tree, a tall bare trunk like a column, with a cluster of branches at the very top."

There was the tennis court, in need of resurfacing after the monsoon, and there was the tree, even taller now, and bushier at the top. The lawns between the house and the court, we noticed, had a low hedge neatly trimmed into scallops, and a small group of palm trees.

Ahead of us was the bungalow, looking very much as it had when we had said "Good-bye" to it all those years before.

"The house, not beautiful or architecturally distinguished, had a pleasant welcoming appearance.

Beneath the cheerfully red-tiled roof, the veranda stretched out each side like welcoming arms."

At the top of the steps a thickset, brown man in well pressed khaki shorts and calf length socks, was waiting to welcome us. It was David K., the Estate Manager. As he held out his hand to greet us, he was joined by Mona, his wife, with whom I had been corresponding, a graceful, smiling young woman, elegant in her flowing Kashmiri dress, who beckoned her children to come forward to meet us.

"Come Samantha, come Sarah," she urged as two pretty children with dark hair and eyes came shyly towards us. "Say 'hello' to Auntie."

I liked that title, and the suggestion that went with it that already I had an acknowledged place in their lives. By coincidence, the children were the same age as we had been when we left.

The taxi driver was waiting to be paid, and before he left he asked David in Tamil if there was any other road he could take back.

"No," David told him, "but it's all down hill. You can just coast down, can't you?" I felt for the unfortunate man, for the light was fading fast, and he would have to find his way along that impossible road in the dark.

So there we were, home at last, but now as guests. The servants bore our luggage away to our rooms, and we were led to the sitting room, which had much to remind us of the way it had been in 1934.

"There is even some of the same furniture." said Mona.

And sure enough, there was the window seat that Mother had had made, and two small tables that appeared in her photographs of the room. Outside on the veranda was the very same rocking chair she had sat in to read to us during our meals.

"And the lilies that never flowered," Mona added, laughing, "they still never flower!"

She had planted them elsewhere in the garden, but as yet they remained flowerless.

Feeling strange and a little as if we were dreaming, we sat on the sofas and over tea and cakes, we discussed how India had changed since we had lived there. Afterwards we were shown our rooms. Mine was the one our parents had had. There was still a dressing table in the window just as there had always been, and there was the cupboard in the wall where Mother had kept the linen, and the matches to which we had secretly helped ourselves to light our biscuit-tin oven while she was playing tennis at the Club.

Peter was in the adjoining room, formerly Father's dressing room, where I had to report first thing every morning to do exercises to stop me walking like a chicken. Peter claimed to have taken part too, but that I did not remember, except for once or twice.

The beds were without the frames that we had had to hold up the mosquito nets, and so far since our arrival in India, we had seen no mosquito nets at all. Nor mosquitoes either, though perhaps that was due to the season. The rooms had many lights, albeit of low wattage and therefore difficult to read by, while the bathrooms had showers and enamelled baths, plus hot as well as cold running water, instead of the wooden tubs we had used, with hot water carried in by Kunichin in a kerosene can.

The bathroom adjoining my (Mother's) room still had a door that opened on to the veranda leading to our old nursery, along which Mother had hurried, stumbling over our toys on the way, when we woke in the night with nightmares, or believed we were being attacked by vampires. Beyond it, the lawn was now planted over with cardamom and other trees, and a covered area where Mona was cultivating anthuriums, whose exotic blooms are sought by flower arrangers.

After we had refreshed ourselves and while Mona was busy preparing the evening meal and putting the children to bed, David showed us round the house. The thing that surprised us most, was the size and height of the rooms; they seemed so much larger than we recalled and now were used differently, in many ways more logically. For instance, the former dining room was now another sittingroom, more often used than the original one. The family now dined in what had been one of the two guest rooms, the bathroom of which was now a kitchen with all the conveniences expected in a modern one; fridge, freezer, washing machine, electric cooker. No need for the food to be carried through the long passage to reach the table.

David and Mona seemed genuinely interested to know how the house had been when we lived there. They had plans to make alterations, and perhaps to restore some of the rooms to their original use.

David's father, an infirm but impressively intelligent eighty-four-year-old occupied the former second guestroom. A servant had been trained to nurse him and attend to his needs. David took us to meet him one evening.

Going Back

"What about Northern Ireland?" was his disconcerting first question. After we had done our best to give him a true picture of that insoluble situation, Peter asked him if he had ever come across Dr Somervell, who in 1932, operating on the dining room table on the front veranda, had removed a large portion of Father's duodenum, thereby probably saving his life.

"I knew him well." the old man said, "He operated on me in 1954. As a matter of fact, I owe my life to him."

It transpired that old Mr K. had suffered paralysis for some time, caused by a tumour on his spine. Dr Somervell performed two operations on him to remove this, one of them taking ten hours. Fortunately it was so successful that Mr K.'s mobility was restored once more, until old age took its toll. With mutual interest we talked about the doctor whose reputation was held in great regard in Travancore, as it was formerly known. As Medical Officer, he had been a member of two expeditions to Everest, in 1931 and 1934, Mallory's last.

The old man was very deaf, and as he seemed to be growing tired, after a while we excused ourselves. The coincidence of his having been treated by the doctor who had saved his and Father's lives, added eerily to my feeling of strangeness about our return.

I did not sleep well in Mother's room, imagining it as it had been and how extraordinary it was to be there. Thinking also, of my own family and that however different our life was in England, to me this place was still home.

As hosts, Mona and David were unsparing in their efforts to take us back to our old haunts,(most had changed almost beyond recognition.) We walked up to the dam with her on the first morning to find the hollow tree in the meadow below the house that had given us so many hours of make-believe, was gone. The water was still pumped up to the bungalow from the dam. There was the pump house where it had always stood, only driven by electric power, instead of the old petrol engine. The wall of the dam had been rebuilt, with a wide chute to carry the water down during the monsoon. We watched children, whose mothers were plucking tea by the reservoir, using the chute as a slide. Everywhere there were plants growing that I recognised, and Mona, a botanist, was able to tell me their names and also the names of the birds we saw. The butterflies were as abundant and as gorgeous they ever had been, fluttering over the tea bushes and lantana.

Below the reservoir, the stream had been dammed in two places, creating two smaller lakes. Gone was the grove of eucalyptus gums that grew by the two-plank bridge below which we used to paddle. Here three year old Ann, on Mother's pony, was thrown into the water when it fell from the bridge. There was now a road across the bridge, wide enough to take a Land Rover. Below it the stream was unchanged from the days when we had played there. Mona told us it was where she took her children to paddle.

Everywhere the hillsides were covered in a thick green quilt of tea interspersed with shade trees, splashed here and there by the bright saris of the workers, and the pale cream and fawn humped cattle that grazed among the bushes. We walked to the hill which we had called the 'Green Hill', where white orchids used to grow, and we would catch grasshoppers or roll over and over down the grassy slopes. Here I had imagined how, when I was grown-up

I would bringing a colony of unemployed people from England to settle, my solution to Britain's employment problem!

There was still a part of it that wasn't cultivated. At its foot there were the graves of the Christian workers, cement coffin-shaped memorials, painted bright blue, red or yellow. The Hindus, because there is a shortage of wood for funeral pyres, bury their dead among the tea, but do not mark the graves.

Peter and I walked up the Green Hill as far as we could, to look at the remembered view across the blue and purple hills but could not get high enough to verify that, as Mother used to claim, it was possible to glimpse the distant sea. In any case the air was misty, and visibility restricted. However, while there we did manage to fulfil one of the purposes of our visit. Mother had often said she would like her ashes scattered there, so we had brought with us a handful of earth from hers and Father's graves, which we sprinkled at a spot like one where we used to pause to look at the view. Now there will always be something of them there.

David had taken us to the top of the next ridge, thinking that was what we meant by 'the Green Hill', through plantations where notices bore the date (1928) when the bushes were first planted under Father's management. The view from the hilltop looking towards High Range, and down a long valley through jungly slopes towards the coast, was breath-takingly beautiful. The thin clouds drifting below us put all into soft focus, blending the greens into the blues and violets. It confirmed my memory of Arnakal as a place of great beauty.
Everywhere we looked we saw change, yet through the

changes, like ghosts, the memories we had treasured in all those years of absence were interposed, like a double exposure on a photograph.

Perhaps the greatest change was in the tea itself, not only in the way it grew but in its manufacture too. David explained the new process and took us to see over the factory one night when they were cutting the leaf. In the dim-lit interior we saw the huge machines, great cylinders that cut and shredded the leaves. Gone were the conveyors, driven by dangerous whirling over-head drive-belts, and the shining brass rollers. Their place was taken by these new, bigger more efficient machines. The tea they now produce, (known as C.T.C., Cut, Torn and Curled) is unlike the tea sold to the Western markets. It is what the Keralese drink, and serve in their restaurants and homes, made with hot milk and plenty of sugar.

"The people are very poor," David explained, "they take it as nourishment rather than refreshment."

Fortunately for Peter and me, the K.s prefer traditional tea, which is still grown in the Nilghiries.

Another change for the better. The workers no longer come to work off their debts, but are well paid, and most have settled on the estate. No longer do naked urchins play outside the grass huts of the lines, or carry their infant siblings while their mothers toil in the fields. They live in brick or cement houses and are sent to school, to learn to read.

The K.s also arranged for Peter to visit the Estate hospital, which as a paediatrician he was keen to see, and to meet the doctor. It was a simple concrete building, equipped to administer first aid for minor accidents or illnesses, heart attacks, maternity or children's diseases,

Going Back

which the doctor was proud to show us, together with the records for infant mortality. Only a small number, but as a percentage shockingly high compared with Britain. Anyone with a serious problem is sent to the nearest large hospital. The Company provides health care free for all the workers and their dependants, including their parents.

I was struck by the authority of David's manner, and his efficiency. Going round the factory he had scarcely to raise a finger for the foreman, or some other worker to spring to his side, eager to carry out his requests. He told us that when he had taken over the Estate six years ago, it had become run down through careless management. "Rule number one," David joked, "the boss must be the boss. And rule number two, the boss is always right even when he's wrong!"

The servants came and went about the house silently on bare feet, offering tea, and removing the used dishes when required. They did not wear uniform, as Francis and Kunichin had. Not for them the white tunic with gleaming brass buttons, and immaculate turban precisely wound into an oval, they wore only the garb that every Indian worker wears, cotton shirt open at the neck and a loincloth.

Mona and David were very amused when we demonstrated the phrases of Tamil that we remembered, embarrassingly confined almost exclusively to commands. "Why," I could not help asking, "were we not at least taught the words for please and thank you?"

I felt, too, how much the Europeans had missed in their refusal to mix on equal terms with the Indians they lived among for so long. No Indians were accepted at the Club, though Anglo-Indians were, which was often not the case in North India. There were a total of twenty-eight

The Tea Planter's Children

Europeans in the District when we lived there. Now there are none but the local Club and the churches are still the social centres. Under Indian Management conditions for the employees appear greatly to have improved, though how much this is due to the Keralese form of Communism, (the only democratically elected Communist government in the world!) is difficult to gauge.

The visit reawakened old memories, and confirmed that on the whole my remembrance was accurate. Sometimes I described to David a scene that I recalled, and nearly always he was able to tell me where that place had been, though sometimes it had been rebuilt elsewhere. This I found very reassuring.

We spent a total of four days with the K.s, moving on to Kodai Kanal and Allepey. David and Mona with typical kindness, as a final gesture, arranged for us to spend an afternoon on the beautiful lake at the Periyar Game Reserve; a memorable experience to take away with us as we said 'Good-bye' to Arnakal for probably the last time

Of my return to Arnakal, my feelings are still mixed, though for the most part, I am glad to have gone, to have laid some old ghosts, made new friends, and come to a fresh understanding of the beautiful place where I was privileged to be born. And glad, too, to see that under the capable management of David and his assistants, Arnakal is prospering. Now a new generation is acquiring memories that they will recall with pleasure in their later years. I am glad I had the opportunity to meet them, and by being there, to have linked my past to their future, even though, sadly, some of my childhood memories are, as I had feared, now less distinct, overlaid by those of our visit.

Printed in the United Kingdom
by Lightning Source UK Ltd.
111084UKS00001B/19-24